Praise

"Simply terrific, with specifics on what lacrosse is all about and how to nurture young athletes."
JILL ALBEE, player, University of New Hampshire; 2nd Team America East All-Conference

"Lacrosse has been a powerful experience and important influence in my life. I'd encourage any kid to give it a try."
SCOTT HOCHSTADT, 3-time All-American player; Coach of the San Francisco Dragons, Major League Lacrosse

"This book will help make lacrosse an exciting experience for your entire family."
JEFFERSON GRIMES, parent of All-Star Team youth player

"I found this book as enjoyable to read as I find lacrosse is to play!"
JUSTIN SMITH, professional player, Philadelphia Barrage; 3-time NCAA College Champion; Division III Player of the Year

"As the mom of three kids, two of them lacrosse players, I am very impressed with the suggestions on how to cope with the highs and the lows that kids go through when playing lacrosse or any sport."
KIM COFFEY, parent, Austin, Texas

"Noah and Melissa show how parents and coaches can have a positive influence on young athletes who are playing lacrosse as well as other sports."
SCOTT AUBIN, lacrosse player and coach

An Important Message to Our Readers

LACROSSE

A Guide for Parents and Players

Noah Fink & **Melissa Gaskill**

A Big Smiling Series Book

Mansion Grove House

Lacrosse: A Guide for Parents and Players

By Noah Fink & Melissa Gaskill

Published by Mansion Grove House

Based Upon The Big Smiling Series Original By Keith Kattan

ISBN-10 1-932421-07-6

ISBN-13 978-1-932421-07-1

Original Content: Copyright © 2006 Noah Fink and Melissa Gaskill

Series Content including Adaptations: Copyright © 2006 Mansion Grove House

Mansion Grove House. PO Box 201734, Austin, TX 78720 USA.

Website: mansiongrovehouse.com

For information on bulk purchases, custom editions and serial rights:
E-mail sales@mansiongrovehouse.com or write us, Attention: Special Sales.

For permission license including reprints, excerpts and quotes: E-mail
permissions@mansiongrovehouse.com or write us, Attention: Permissions.

Printed in the United States of America

Library of Congress Cataloging-in-Publication Data

Fink, Noah.
  Lacrosse : a guide for parents and players / Noah Fink and Melissa Gaskill.
      p. cm. -- (A big smiling series book)
  Includes bibliographical references and index.
  ISBN 1-932421-07-6 (pbk. : alk. paper)
  1. Lacrosse--United States. I. Gaskill, Melissa. II. Title.
GV989.F55 2006
796.34'7--dc22

2006035108

Big Smiling Lacrosse Team!

Acquisition, Permissions & Reviews: **Maureen Malliaras**

Cover Designer: **Bill Carson**

Content Design: **Aesthetics Company**

Copy Editor: **Judie Lewellen**

Illustrator: **Ryan MacMurray**

Marketing Development: **Laura Duncan**

Credits: See Appendix "Credits"

About Noah & Melissa

Noah Fink played collegiate lacrosse at Bucknell University and is now the head lacrosse coach at the University of Texas. In his three years, the team has won the Lone Star Alliance twice and represented the league in the National Tournament. He went to graduate school at the University of California, San Diego and began his coaching career there, for the Torrey Pines and Coronado High School lacrosse teams. Noah actively supports the growth of lacrosse in his local community and runs youth leagues.

Melissa Gaskill, parent of three active children, has served as coach, volunteer and fan for various youth sports, including lacrosse. A prolific professional writer, Melissa shares her experiences with readers for national publications such as Family Fun and The Nature Conservancy, as well as in many regional publications. She wrote a weekly parenting column, The Children's Connection, for six years.

Contents

Introduction

Sports in general, and lacrosse in particular, offer many benefits for your kids such as the opportunity to make friends, build character, and improve physical fitness. Playing an organized sport can give kids a positive outlet, a place to fit in at school, motivation to do well, and opportunities to travel for tournaments and camps. Sports can even potentially mean money for college and influence career choices.

Whether you know the game of lacrosse or not, whether your child is eight or 18, experienced or just starting out, this book is your guide to all that lacrosse has to offer and how to have the best possible experience with the sport. This book gives practical advice on everything from getting started on that first team and what equipment you'll need, to leveraging lacrosse to help with college admissions and maybe even a career in the pros. It's written from the perspective of a parent and a player and coach.

As a parent, I (Melissa) was eager and supportive when my three children first showed an interest in organized sports. Like many parents, I had visions of grandeur on the field and occasional fantasies of full-ride scholarships to college. I also liked the idea of getting the kids off the couch and outside. But I quickly learned that organized sports have changed in recent years, and the experience isn't always a positive one for kids or their families. I discovered it is important to consider why your child wants to play sports, and to find coaches who believe sports should be fun and that all kids should get to play.

I heard too many stories about young children being pushed beyond their developmental abilities, kids getting injuries at young ages, poor coaching, win-at-all-costs attitudes that forget the kids, burnout and other problems. One reason I wanted to write this book was to remind parents that kids are kids, and childhood is supposed to be fun. Fortunately, enjoying a sport and being really good at it aren't mutually exclusive goals.

My kids have played t-ball, baseball, kickball, softball, volleyball, soccer, football, lacrosse and ultimate Frisbee. They've played on recreational, select and school teams. Their father and I have coached a time or two, worked as team parents, served on boards, and been their number one fans. We've supported the kids in trying new sports, and when they decided that things weren't working out. For us, playing sports was always about the kids - what they wanted, what they enjoyed, what was right for them. It wasn't ever a way to live vicariously, earn bragging rights, or chase a scholarship. We made sure that school came first, that we didn't sacrifice family life for sports, and that the kids had plenty of other interests to help them on their way to becoming well-rounded, happy and healthy adults.

Because lacrosse is still a relatively new sport in our home state of Texas, when two of our kids took an interest in it, I had some learning to do. Fortunately, coaches and other parents were more than happy to help. There were books about how to play the sport, and how to coach it, but not one that gave parents all the angles - basics of the game, equipment, conditioning and coaching, levels of play, college issues, and even the professional level. That's another reason for writing this one.

As a player and coach, I (Noah) was interested in passing on my love of the game to the next generation, introducing young people - and their families - to a sport I'm passionate about, and that has been a positive influence on my life. I was introduced to lacrosse in the seventh grade and haven't put my stick down yet.

Lacrosse is truly a game that offers everything most people want in a sport. It is fast-paced and action-packed, yet involves a high level of strategy and skill. While it involves some hitting and contact, the better players focus more on quick ball movement and speed in order to get the ball up the field and score goals.

A kid can pick up a stick and within a few days be proficient enough to step onto the field and play a game. Mastering the game, however, takes years, and usually players are still learning the finer points even after their bodies can no longer keep up with the speed of the game. The most passionate and intelligent players can be found playing in the masters divisions around the country, all still wearing the same childish grin as when they first picked up that stick.

Lacrosse is exploding around the country and is no longer a sport you pick up just because your parents didn't play. The small and close-knit lacrosse community that once thrived in pockets of the country has grown, and it is only a matter of time before the sport reaches a level of popularity that early players only dreamed of. I would like people to learn some of the basics from this book, but more importantly, to recognize what it means to be a member of the lacrosse community.

Lacrosse and its spirit have been a bright spot in the world of sports. Players from all over the country, even the world, are linked by some kind of bond and by friendship. As lacrosse grows, coaches will need to hold fast to those values of sportsmanship and fair play. I hope parents will also stress these positive values. Then we can keep what is special about lacrosse alive and thriving.

Melissa and I sat down to write a book that will help parents teach and encourage their children. All kids can learn to excel and enjoy lacrosse, given the proper instruction and support. Sure, being the fastest player is great. But any type of player with the proper motivation, encouragement and coaching can play the game and play it well. Learning to play this sport well will translate into a set of life skills that will help your child succeed in any endeavor he or she may choose.

Our main goal is to give parents all the information they need to support their kids in lacrosse. If your kids aren't currently playing, we hope you'll encourage them to try this exciting, growing sport that can take you places and provide hours of fun and enjoyment. We hope this book will help you discover how to make lacrosse part of your life.

Noah Fink   Melissa Gaskill
noah@mansiongrovehouse.com   melissa@mansiongrovehouse.com

Common Acronyms

ILF	International Lacrosse Federation
MLL	Major League Lacrosse
NATA	National Athletic Trainers Association
NCAA	National Collegiate Athletic Association
NFHS	National Federation of State High School Associations
NJCAA	National Junior College Athletic Association
NLL	National Lacrosse League
NSCA	National Strength and Conditioning Association
PCA	Positive Coaching Alliance

1

The Fastest Game On Two Feet

"Lacrosse is a gift from the creator."
Native American belief

You may have picked up this book because your son or daughter came home the other day and said "I want to play lacrosse." All you could reply was "What the heck is lacrosse?" Or, maybe you saw a lacrosse practice on the neighborhood soccer field and thought, that looks like a fun game. It could be your neighbor's kid has been playing the game and loving it, and you wonder if the same would be true for your child.

Even if you once played lacrosse yourself, maybe you could now use a little help getting your child into the game. Whatever your reason for wanting a book about lacrosse, you've picked the right one and at the right time, too. The sport, which has a long history and is rich in tradition, is bursting onto the national and international scene in a big way.

People in Canada, the northeastern United States and a few other areas around the world have been huge fans for decades, and now the sport is spreading far and wide. Many of us are getting acquainted with lacrosse for the first time, and finding it exciting.

This book will explain the basics of lacrosse, help you decide if it is right for your kids, show you where and how they can get started playing, and walk you through everything else you as a parent need to know in order for your child to play and enjoy the game.

America's First Team Sport

Ask a player why lacrosse is his favorite sport and you'll likely get an earful, starting with how the game is rooted in tradition. Native American tribes were playing it when Europeans arrived in the 1600s. In fact, it's one of the few pieces of native culture that survived and eventually prospered through the influx of immigrants to the Americas.

Lacrosse had spiritual significance for Native Americans. It was a game they played to show gratitude to their creator, to show respect for honored members of their nation, or to settle a dispute between two tribes. Early lacrosse teams could consist of hundreds or even thousands of players, the goals might be miles apart and the game could last as long as three days. Each community had its own style of play with variations on the basic equipment, attire and associated ceremonies. Young men prepared for the game the same way they prepared for war. The game taught the men lessons about courage, strength, honor, respect and fair play.

In what is now southern Ontario and western New York, the six tribes of the Iroquois Nation first established the limitation to 12 or 15 players and defined field boundaries. While modern lacrosse varies in some ways from the ancient game, its spiritual roots and the importance of proper conduct still survive.

European settlers in what is now Canada took to the local game and helped make it the thriving sport that it is there today. Lacrosse is the oldest continually played sport in North America. In fact, lacrosse is one of the national sports of Canada; the other is ice hockey. The rules of hockey, in fact, are patterned after lacrosse, and many hockey players are also avid lacrosse players.

Lacrosse has been popular for many years in the northeast United States, especially in Maryland and New York. It's been big in states such as California and Ohio for many years, and is now gaining in popularity across the country. The game is also catching on around the world, as athletes in Europe, Japan, New Zealand and many other countries discover the fun and excitement of lacrosse.

Why Lacrosse?

Lacrosse is an extremely active game. Things move fast on the field, so your kids won't be standing around or getting bored. Parents won't get bored watching, either, although you may be confused initially since the rules are sometimes tough to grasp and the stick checks can look scary at first.

The game involves a depth of teamwork which helps kids develop good rapport with their fellow players. On the other hand, kids can also work on specific skills for the game by themselves.

These include wall ball, where players throw a ball against a wall and catch it with the stick; cradling, or carrying the ball in the pocket; and scooping the ball off the ground. All of these, especially wall ball, are encouraged and even required by coaches of all age groups, including college. Prepare to get completely fed up with your kids when they start doing some or all of these things in the house!

Lacrosse is also a sport where size isn't all that important. Anyone who is quick and athletic, boys and girls alike, can learn to play lacrosse. This is a safe sport as well. Many of the game's rules and league policies, and the equipment players wear, from boy's helmets to girl's goggles, are designed to prevent injuries. In fact, lacrosse has fewer injuries overall than football or soccer, according to NCAA statistics. Parents have little to worry about if their kids are taught proper technique, wear the right equipment and, of course, follow the rules.

Finally, lacrosse can take your kid lots of places. More and more high schools now have teams, as do many colleges. High school and college teams are traveling across the country and even internationally to play in games and tournaments. Even if your child doesn't play lacrosse in college, participation could help him get into a college since a long-term commitment to a sport will look good on a college application.

Players can even aspire to playing on a professional team. Major League Lacrosse (More info: majorleaguelacrosse.com), begun in 2001, has six teams with four in the planning stage. The National Lacrosse League (More info: nll.com), founded as the current organization in 1987, has 11 professional indoor teams in two divisions in the United States and Canada. The opportunities for coaching and officiating at the middle and high school level and at college are growing every year. The number of lacrosse camps also continues to grow, as does their need for coaches and officials.

Learning about Lacrosse

Whether your child is already interested in lacrosse and you want to catch up, or if you are intrigued and want your child to consider this sport, you want to learn more. The best way to learn a sport, of course, is to play it.

While most parents never had that chance, you don't have to be a player to enjoy watching lacrosse, and you don't have to know much about the game for your child to get into it. The very fact that Mom and Dad are clueless about the sport can add greatly to its appeal for youngsters, especially teens who love knowing something their parents don't.

Start by watching a few games at the local high school or college. Ask a fan or parent, or your kids if they are driving your interest, to explain the basics to you. (You'll find game basics at the end of this chapter.) If you want to get your child interested, take her along once you think you have the general idea. You may be surprised at how quickly kids pick up on the game. After all, many of them understand soccer, hockey and other sports with similarities, and kids seem to love that cool, mystical Native American element. Very soon, your child may be explaining the action to you.

Just remember that young children have short attention spans. If yours is wandering off to pick clover by half-time, or wants to go by the local drive-in for a milk shake before the game ends, that's okay. Make the time that you watch together a priority. Turn off your cell phone, put down the newspaper and give your child and the game your full attention.

Watch a Camp Session

If your child is interested in the game, one of the best ways to check out lacrosse is to take him to watch a session at a summer or holiday camp. These sessions tend to be filled with enthusiastic kids who love the game. In a camp setting, the emphasis is generally off winning and on having fun.

Kids learn a lot by watching, too, and you might be surprised at how much technique your child picks up this way. Of course, watching a high school or college tournament is also fun, and a healthy, competitive environment can add excitement to the game. But an emphasis on who wins and who loses - which you are more likely to run into at high school and college-level games - is not what you want at this point.

You also never know when a game might get intense and frustrated players or their fans might mutter something inappropriate for tender young ears. To keep your child from getting the wrong message about this game or sports in general, look for relaxed settings initially, such as camps, or early season practice at your local high school or recreational league.

When you do watch the more competitive levels of play, talk with your youngsters about the appropriate role of competition, and the importance of being graceful winners and losers. With young kids, be prepared to keep them entertained with sideline activities if there are lulls in the action on the field (although there won't be many), or if their attention starts to wander.

Read Up

There are a few good books on lacrosse out there, though they aren't specifically geared to kids. You can share a book about the history and background of the sport with your child with these two: *Lacrosse: North America's Game* and *Lacrosse: A History of the Game.* Several magazines about the sport are also readily available.

Look for: *Inside Lacrosse* (More info: insidelacrosse.com), *Lacrosse Magazine* (More info: uslacrosse.org) and *e-lacrosse.com*, an on-line magazine that has video content as well as print articles.

Games Off the Field

Get a feel for what lacrosse is all about by playing around with a lacrosse stick and ball. Wall ball, which is nothing more than tossing a ball against a wall and catching it, is fun for kids and one of the best ways to develop the throwing and catching skills essential in lacrosse.

If you have a high wall on your house—a windowless one - you can do this at home. The side of a gym wall at your neighborhood school or the backboard at a tennis court will also work well. Playing wall ball in a racquetball court is ideal, as the wall is smooth and the ball's bounces will be less unpredictable.

Make up games, such as seeing how long you can keep wall ball going without missing or dropping a ball, or playing to music. The wall in an enclosed area is a great place to practice this without the frustration of constantly chasing the ball down the street. Right from the start, make sure that your child is throwing and catching with both hands. Good lacrosse players must be able to handle the stick and ball equally well with the right and the left hands.

Shooting on goal, either with an actual lacrosse goal or one of the trainer aids available, is also fun. Kids always like to score goals. Again, using both hands right from the start will pay huge dividends in the long run.

An old-fashioned game of catch, using lacrosse sticks and a lacrosse ball instead of gloves and a baseball, is a great way to have fun and improve eye-hand coordination at the same time. These can also be spiced up a bit by moving farther away from each other or adding a "keep away" element.

If you have trees in your yard or in a nearby park, turn them into lacrosse defenders and play tree dodging. Kids can set up a goal or pick a spot to serve as goal then run through the trees, dodging them as if they were players trying to take the ball, switching hands and adding other stick work as they improve.

Volunteer

Put yourself in the middle of the action by offering to be the time keeper or score keeper at games for your local recreational league, middle or high school. This allows you to watch games, meet players the age of your child, and get to know parents whose kids are already playing and enjoying lacrosse.

Once your child is on a team, sign up to be the team parent - teams always need parents to bring water and healthy snacks, line the fields, help arrange carpools, and to provide positive sideline cheering at games.

Lacrosse Vacation

Travel to one of the cities with a professional lacrosse team and take in a game. If you are traveling near a university or college, check its website to see if it has a lacrosse team and catch a college-level game. One of the most exciting events in U.S. lacrosse is the Final Four, which takes place every Memorial Day weekend in various locations.

More than 45,000 people attended the 2005 Final Four, enjoying great men's and women's lacrosse in an upbeat environment. The Lacrosse World Cup is another big event in the sport—it's a major showdown among top teams from all over the world, and is held in various locations, such as England, Japan and Australia. At the 2005 event in Baltimore, Maryland, ten teams competed - Australia, Canada, Czech Republic, England, Germany, Japan, New Zealand, Scotland, the U.S., and Wales (More info: uslacrosse.org).

Take a couple of balls and a pair of sticks on your next family vacation. Play catch on the beach - you might attract a crowd of lacrosse fans.

Game Basics

Understanding the basics of lacrosse makes it more fun to watch, plus it will help you support and encourage your child in the sport. Some people compare lacrosse to a combination of hockey and soccer played with sticks. The game does have elements similar to other sports, but really, lacrosse is a unique game. The basics, though, are fairly simple.

Men's Lacrosse

Men's lacrosse is played between two teams on a field 110 yards long, divided into halves by a midfield line. Each end has a 40-yard box called the restraining box, offensive zone or defensive zone. There is a 6-foot by 6-foot goal at each end of the field, surrounded by a circle called the crease. Teams include ten players: one goaltender or goalie, three defensemen, three midfielders or middies, and three attackmen.

Attackmen coordinate the offense and generally stay on the offensive side of the field. They use short sticks to minimize their chances of losing the ball. Defensemen guard the opponent's attackmen and try to take the ball away from them. They use a longer stick and generally stay on the defensive half of the field.

Midfielders, also called middies, play both offense and defense and so run the entire length of the field.

Substitutions are more frequent for middies since they are running more than the other players. Most middies play with shorter sticks than the other players, but one of them can use a longer defense stick, and that player is known as the long stick midfielder, or LSM.

Play begins with a face-off at the center of the midfield line. Two middies kneel with the head of their sticks together and the ball in between. At the whistle, each tries to get possession of the ball or get it to a teammate. Players are not allowed to touch the ball with their hands at any time, but kicking the ball is legal, even into the goal, although kicking a stick is not.

When the ball goes out of bounds, normally possession is awarded to the team that did not touch it last. On a shot, though, possession is given to the player closest to the ball when it leaves the field. It is for this reason you will often see players racing after the ball following a missed shot, holding their sticks out, trying to win possession by being closest to the ball.

During play, each team must keep any four players in its defensive half of the field and three in the offensive half, or be called offsides. Offensive players may not step into the crease, that circle around the goal, in their offensive half of the field. Defensive players may step in the crease, but not carry the ball into it.

Players are allowed to check, or hit, the player with the ball and any player within 5 yards of a loose ball. Players can check with the body or the stick; when body checking, the player cannot make contact above the shoulders, below the waist or from the rear, and must have both hands on his own stick. Stick checks must be on the opponent's stick or gloves. While you will see lots of checks on the arms and sides, they will not be called penalties if the defender had a chance of hitting the stick or glove but the offensive player moved his stick or spun so the check landed elsewhere. Players may never cross-check, which is using the part of the stick held between the gloves.

Youth games typically are 32 minutes long, with eight minute quarters; high school games are 48 minutes long with 12 minute quarters; and collegiate games are 60 minutes long with 15 minute quarters. There are two-minute breaks between quarters and a ten-minute break at half time. Teams change sides between periods.

There are two kinds of penalties, personal and technical fouls. Personal fouls put the player in the penalty box for one minute and include slashing, tripping, illegal body checks, cross-checking, and unnecessary roughness. Unsportsmanlike conduct, such as fighting, results in being removed from the game. An illegal stick is also a personal foul (More info: Chapter 2. Information on regulations for equipment) for which a player may be given a three-minute penalty.

Technical fouls are more procedural in nature; offsides, delay of game, pushing with possession, interference and so forth. These may result in loss of possession or 30 seconds in the penalty box, depending on whether the team had possession when the infraction occurred.

Women's Lacrosse

Women's lacrosse is played with 11 players on each team; five on attack, five defenders and a goalkeeper. Attack positions are first, second and third home, and attack wings. First home position is located in front of the goal, and her responsibility is to score. Second home is considered the playmaker, and the third home transitions the ball from defense to attack. Wings are also responsible for the transition from defense to attack.

Defense positions include point, who marks, or covers, the other teams' first home; coverpoint, who marks second home; third man, who marks third home; and center, who controls the draw and plays both defense and attack. Defense wings are responsible for marking the attack wings and bringing the ball into the attack area. The goalkeeper, of course, protects the goal. In the face-off, the ball is held between the back of two players' sticks above the ground until the ref blows a whistle.

Women's high school games last 50 minutes or two 25-minutes halves, and collegiate games 60 minutes, in two 30-minute halves. The field had no measured boundaries until a rule change which established hard boundaries but allowed some flexibility with a maximum playing area of 140 by 70 yards and a minimum area of 110 by 60 yards. The only legal checks are stick to stick, directed away from the player with the ball and seven inches from her head. No body checking is allowed, and so the only protective gear required for women is goggles and a mouth-guard, and gloves for goalies. The requirement for goggles is relatively new, in fact, and many female players are still getting used to it.

Fouls are categorized as major or minor, and the penalty is a "free position." For major fouls, the offending player is placed four meters behind the player taking the free position. For a minor foul, the offending player is placed four meters off, in the direction from which she approached her opponent before committing the foul. After positioning, play is resumed.

Box Lacrosse

Common in Canada, box lacrosse is played indoors on an artificial turf called the carpet. Most games are played in an area 200 by 85 feet, although this can vary some depending on the arena. Box lacrosse has six players, versus 10 for field lacrosse. Sticks are shorter and the goal is smaller, although the goalie wears more protective gear.

Box lacrosse players are often also hockey players, with obvious ramifications. The National Lacrosse League of Canada plays box lacrosse.

For a complete copy of men's and women's rules, see uslacrosse.org.

This basic information on the fastest sport on two feet may have you ready to get your kids out on the field. You'll find information on the gear that lacrosse players need in the next chapter and guidance on finding teams, coaches and camps in subsequent chapters. You and your players are going to have a lot of fun!

2

Gearing Up

"If I was in charge, I'd require everyone to use a wooden stick."
Leah Dubie, former player, Hofstra University, and
lacrosse coach

A flood of technology, innovation and competition between manufacturers has turned the sport on its head. "The wall of a lacrosse retailer is now full of components and options for players desiring a competitive edge" says Patrick Gowan, a retailer and lacrosse defenseman.

The Virtues of Value

Before your kids can play lacrosse, they'll need the proper gear. The game actually involves a fair amount of the stuff, especially for boys. The gear doesn't make the lacrosse player, of course, but the right pieces can help your player perform better and have a more fun game.

As in many sports, gear also protects players from injury. Outfitting your child with lacrosse gear will cost anywhere from $200 to $500, depending on quality of the gear and the age of your player. Expect to be on the lower end of the scale if you are outfitting a daughter instead of a son.

The best equipment isn't necessarily the most expensive, but on the other hand, cheap gear can end up costing you more if your child gets hurt or if you have to replace inadequate pads or a broken stick. Use this chapter to get acquainted with lacrosse equipment and what it is meant to do before you open up your wallet.

Where to Buy

These days, you can probably get the best lacrosse equipment deals on the Internet. The drawback to shopping online, especially for those just starting out, is that players can't try on or try out gear - at least not without a lot of back and forth shipping costs. If you aren't sure what type or size glove your child really needs, for example, nothing beats being able to look at, feel and try on a wide selection.

Because lacrosse is still a fairly new sport in many places, the general sports equipment stores probably won't have a big selection, or a staff who know much about the game. Stores that specialize in lacrosse are becoming more common, though, and while you might think these would be more expensive, that isn't usually the case.

These stores offer good value, staff members who know the game and will get to know your child, with ongoing service after the sale, including pocket re-stringing services. They can help you buy the right gear the first time around, which could save you money. Some have rental programs, a good option for those trying the sport for the first time, and some deal in used equipment, which is a great way to equip your child if you aren't sure yet whether he'll stick with (no pun intended) the sport.

The guidance and advice available at a store specializing in lacrosse has proved invaluable for many parents, like Kim Coffey of Austin, Texas, whose two boys took up lacrosse in the third and fifth grades after seeing a demonstration at their school. "They had never played lacrosse and it wasn't a sport we parents knew anything about, so we did not have any equipment except cleats," says Coffey.

"We were lost and had no idea what the boys needed." The staff at a local lacrosse store guided the family through equipment purchases for the boys as beginners, and continued to help as the boys grew and their equipment needs changed.

Mail order catalogs are an option for repeat purchases, replacement gear and accessories. They offer a wide selection and, typically, good prices, and are usually run by lacrosse players or former players. Major lacrosse catalog vendors that have been around for a while include Warrior, STX, Brine, Gait, Debeer and Cascade. All of these have numerous products on the market and will customize goods for teams. Companies newer to the market, like Harrow and Riddell, have increased the options for consumers.

Buy to Last, or Not

Most lacrosse gear will generally last about two years. That said, you will run across players who have played with the same favorite pair of gloves all through high school and college. The most common reason for replacing gear is because a player has outgrown it. For growing kids, it is important to make sure pads fit properly to ensure safe play.

Kids want to look the part, of course, with the "cool" stuff, and in most cases, if you want to indulge them, go ahead. It can add to the overall appeal of the sport to look the part, and lacrosse is definitely about being cool. Just beware of getting caught up with the "must-have" new products that come out every year. If your kids want the really cool gear and statement clothes, why not let them earn it? Use the old-fashioned, tried and true methods like babysitting and mowing lawns, or reward them for getting to practice on time, putting in extra time on the wall, or taking good care of the gear they have.

Maybe award some points for taking a pass on the junk food. Or, offer to buy the cool gear when she completes a tournament or improves her running time. Just avoid offering rewards for outcomes; telling your kid you'll buy the hot shoes if she scores more goals than a teammate is a bad idea.

For essential gear, make some smart choices. Some equipment will be outgrown or is expected to wear out and be replaced more often, and going with top-of-the-line doesn't make much sense there. With other pieces, higher quality does make sense, either because the quality makes a real difference on the field, or because the equipment should last longer or be more durable. In the explanations of equipment provided here, there are guidelines about whether to aim higher or lower on the price scale, and why.

The Fit

The key to selecting all equipment should be good fit and appropriate quality. No matter what the cost, the equipment needs to fit well to provide the proper protection, and make certain your player is comfortable. Fit is most important with gloves, which need to fit snugly but allow mobility, and arm pads, which cover the elbow. Arm pads that are too big will slide down, exposing the elbow.

Fit is less important with shoulder pads, which will typically be worn under a t-shirt or jersey. Helmets and goggles need to fit well, too, so they don't move around and impair vision or compromise safety.

Quality Means Safety

Quality is basically about safety, although it contributes to playing well, too. It matters more with some pieces of equipment than others. Lacrosse is a contact sport and involves checking, at least for boys, with the body and with the stick. Rules require that stick checks be on the opponent's stick or glove, which makes those gloves critical pieces of protection.

Lesser-quality gloves may not provide adequate protection, resulting in bruised or even broken fingers. It is easy to test whether a glove provides good protection - put it on and rap the back of the hand with a lacrosse stick (carefully, of course). Checks inevitably will land on other parts of the body, especially elbows and shoulders, so the pads protecting these areas are important, too.

The Gear

Starter sets of all the basic equipment are pretty widely available for both boys and girls.

Starter Sets

Boys' sets usually include arm pads, shoulder pads, gloves, mouth guard, and ball. Helmet and stick may be included or sold separately. Girls' sets have goggles, mouth guard, and ball and usually include a basic stick.

Starter sets may seem like a good idea for beginners, and certainly make that first shopping trip easier for parents, but they may not always be the best choice. Sets are most appropriate and the best deal for younger players who are not yet in middle school. But starter gear is typically of the less-expensive and lesser quality variety, and for older players, middle school and above, starter sets may last only three to six months before your child will be dragging you back to the store for a new set of gloves or arm pads with more protection and comfort. Starter sets are almost always appropriate for girls' equipment unless the team orders goggles in bulk, in which case the starter set might be duplication.

Sometimes, the drive to get newer and more expensive equipment is the desire, by both boys and girls, to have the latest and most technologically advanced product. Starter sets, though, likely remain the best deal for those players testing out the sport who will likely outgrow equipment by the end of their first year.

Sticks

The stick is "the thing" in lacrosse. After all, the name - lacrosse - comes from the French for "hooked stick". Many parents wonder if their child's lacrosse stick has become permanently attached to the body. It will show up at the dinner table, in the car and probably even next to the bed of a player who has really fallen for the game. This is a good thing.

Lacrosse sticks have three parts: the shaft or handle, the head, and the pocket. You can buy complete sticks, or each of the parts, with assembly included or done on your own. A girl's stick is typically sold complete and almost always with a head that is already strung. Girls' sticks are

42-inches long and have shallower pockets and, since girls have more highly refined taste (sorry, guys), are available in a variety of colors.

Boys' sticks are starting to vary more in color to appeal to the creative and flashy players. With more experience, your child is likely to want to exchange a basic shaft for a composite or titanium one that is lighter, stronger, and more comfortable in play. For boys, there are attack sticks, which must be 40- to 42-inches long, and defense sticks, which are six feet long.

Shaft

Beginning players should learn the game with a short shaft, then, if they play defense, switch to a longer shaft later. Some younger players cut down the shaft to a shorter length to make the stick more manageable. Shorter lengths do not meet rules for high school or college-level play, however.

Choosing a handle boils down to balancing weight against strength or durability. Less expensive shafts are made from aluminum alloys, which are lightweight but not very durable. These are good for players just starting out. You obviously don't want your kid trying to play with a stick he can barely lift.

The most durable handles are titanium, which although very durable can be heavy, and are probably the most expensive on the market. Somewhere in-between is probably best for most young players. Carbon composite and aluminum alloy shafts can be found in numerous weights, grips and colors. It is helpful to visit a store where your player can hold and handle different types of shafts.

Girls' sticks don't have to be as durable as boys', since their lacrosse involves less checking, and generally girls will prefer a lighter weight and matching colors. With the exception of basic aluminum shafts, most will come with a one-year warranty.

Head

Made of molded plastic, stick heads vary in overall width, shape, design of the top and sidewalls, and ball stop. These variations can make a difference in performance, but some of them are simply personal preference. Wider heads are best for beginning players, because these make it easier to catch the ball. Beginners should also choose a head with a flatter top, or scoop, for handling ground balls with more ease.

More skilled players prefer narrower heads with an offset, which provide greater ball control and ball protection, and increased shooting and passing accuracy. The shape and angle of the sidewalls, which affect ground balls and handling, will be less important for beginning players. Additional holes in the side rails offer more options for stringing.

Some heads have over-molding where the head is attached to the shaft, intended to reduce ball rattle and spin. The newest designs feature an off-set head or shaft, which is supposed to improve "feel" and ball control. You'll see lots of ads in lacrosse magazines and websites for sticks with these angled heads. There is spirited debate within the sport about this and other technological advances in equipment, just as there is ongoing debate in many sports about the changes technology brings and what it means to individual athletes, performance, records and many other aspects of competition.

Collegiate men's rules require that the stick pass a "table top" test; when resting on a table with the pocket opening facing down, the distance from the table to the highest edge of the head cannot exceed 2 3/4 inches. Most heads, with the exception of beginner products, should have a one-year warranty. Keep in mind that many manufacturers are now pushing the limits of what is legal for play. Maintenance becomes especially important with sticks that are close to that legal line.

Pockets

There are two basic types of pockets, mesh (which can be hard or soft) and traditional. The latter has leather strips running lengthwise on the pocket. It is a matter of personal preference which to use, although the traditional pocket is more difficult to adjust and maintain. Soft mesh can be best for beginners, but hard mesh is more popular with most experienced players, as the pockets tend to remain consistent for the longest time.

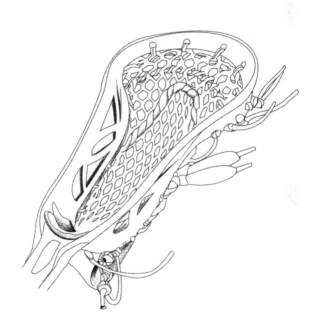

Mesh with wider holes, known as monster or six diamond mesh, has become popular but is not significantly different from regular, old-fashioned hard mesh. There is also variation in where the throwing strings are on a pocket. Some players prefer tighter throwing strings, which can increase "whip" or the speed of a shot, but can be difficult to handle. Again, this boils down mostly to personal preference and what a player gets used to. Pocket variations, such as corner pockets and "pita"

pockets, have been developed and became popular with players in recent years.

Anyone who plays lacrosse for any length of time will end up needing to re-string a pocket, because the mesh stretches out and eventually breaks. Although stores or the team stick doctor will do this, for a fee, it is a good idea for your child to learn how to re-string. Re-stringing kits and materials are widely available. See if a coach or more experienced player is willing to help your child learn this skill. Resist the temptation to learn yourself; real lacrosse players string their own pockets. If you just can't help yourself, get your own stick.

Balls

In regulation games, boys' lacrosse uses white balls and girls' uses yellow ones. For practices and training, a variety of colors are available, and a distinctive color makes it easier to identify yours. Soft training balls are also available and are easier on fragile items around the house. Every serious lacrosse player can boast about breaking at least a few windows.

Gloves

Unless you are buying replacement gloves identical to the pair already in use, it is best to have your child try on gloves and handle a stick while wearing them. There should be a little room at the end of the fingers, but not much. Gloves need to be pretty snug to provide the best protection and handling, and need to allow for a good range of motion, otherwise your player may have trouble gripping and handling the stick.

The technology has improved, with newer gloves providing a better feel for the stick. The palm of the glove should be made of durable material. Newer designs have vents so that the glove "breathes" and the player's hands are more comfortable. Some gloves provide more wrist protection than others; your player's need for this will depend somewhat on the level of play.

Gloves are available for girls, but are optional. Gloves will provide some protection from potential injury, since accidental hits from a stick or another player's body is certainly possible in girls' lacrosse. Gloves will also keep a player's hands warm in cold weather, although three-quarter finger designs are available for warmer weather play. Sizes range from extra small to extra large.

Men's Glove Sizing Chart	
Size in Inches	**Age / Weight**
10	5-8 years old or 71-90 pounds
12	9-13 years old or 91-140 pounds
13	14+ years old or 140+ pounds

Arm Pads and Elbow Pads

Arm pads are intended to protect the arm and elbow. Typically, attack and mid-fielders wear arm pads that are longer and provide more protection, while defense players wear shorter pads that just cover the elbow - since they are the ones throwing checks and not getting hit. Some designs have hard plastic caps over the elbow, while others have thick padding.

Arm pads need to fit snugly so when a player runs or throws the ball, they don't slide down the arm. Most are designed with Velcro straps above and below the elbow to hold them in place. Ventilation is important in warmer climates. Choose pads that fit well and allow for good mobility. Plan on buying several pairs of these as your player grows.

Shoulder Pads

Lacrosse shoulder pads are mostly designed to protect players from errant stick checks and from some body checks. Lacrosse has few big hits like the kind you see in football, one of the reasons some parents like this sport. These pads are more lightweight than those used in football. Players in positions that take more checks, like attack, will need pads that provide more protection than those in other positions. The crucial spot to check for adequate padding is the bone on top of the shoulder.

Comfort is also important, which is affected by the weight of the pads and range of motion they allow. Some players prefer pads that come almost midway down the torso, while others like shorter pads. Most shoulder pads cover the chest and back with thicker padding on top of the shoulder and removable pads extending from the shoulder over the upper arm. There are also vest-type pads that are lighter weight and provide minimal protection, usually without the upper arm pads.

Shoulder Pad Sizing Chart	
Size	**Age / Weight**
XS	under five years of age and 70 pounds
S	6-8 years old, 71-100 pounds
M	9-13 years old, 91-140 pounds
L	over 14, 141-170 pounds
XL	over 14 and 170 pounds

Rib Pads

These are optional pads, worn below the shoulder pads, that wrap around either side of the body to protect ribs from blows. Players may also wear these while healing from an injury to the ribs. The lightweight pads are held in place with straps over the shoulder, which are adjustable in length. Choose based on fit, comfort and mobility.

Helmets

Helmets are made of durable plastic and are intended to protect the head and face from stick and body checks, and from the ball. Again, they are lighter weight than football helmets. The helmet surrounds the top and back of the head and covers the chin, and a face mask protects the face. Important considerations in choosing a helmet are fit, visibility and comfort.

A helmet should not move around when a player runs, and it should offer maximum peripheral vision. To date, most players have worn helmets by Cascade, but Warrior, Brine and Riddell have come out with competitive alternatives. Check with *Consumer Reports* (More info: consumerreports.org) and lacrosse retailers about which helmets offer the best protection.

Lacrosse teams will often color-coordinate by purchasing custom helmets, so check with your coach before buying one.

Shoes

Lacrosse players wear cleated shoes. The type of cleat depends on the playing surface, although metal spikes, like those worn by baseball players, are not allowed. Generally, football or soccer cleats will work for lacrosse. Some shoe manufacturers have begun to make specific lacrosse cleats. Sets of replacement cleats allow players to alter shoes to accommodate a variety of playing surfaces.

Good fit is critical, as is comfort and support. Shoes, after all, support the entire body and lacrosse is an active sport with a lot of running. Some players like a three-quarter or mid-top shoe to provide ankle support. Some also use heel gels or insoles for additional support and cushioning. This can be particularly important for players in growth-spurt mode, as running can cause some pain in the growing heel. Don't buy shoes with "room to grow," as proper fit is important. Check regularly to make sure your player hasn't outgrown the shoes.

Socks are recommended, as wearing shoes without socks can lead to athlete's foot or other problems. Encourage your player to wash socks after every use to avoid both unpleasant odors and worse things, like athlete's foot. All pads should be washed regularly as well.

Other Equipment

Mouth guards are required in lacrosse, for both boys and girls. These should be the type that you heat and mold to the player's mouth. Some mouth guards offer dental warranties, and certain brands work better for children with braces. Packing an extra mouth guard in the gear bag is a good idea, as this small piece of equipment is easy to misplace.

Athletic cups are optional for boys, although highly recommended for goalies. Sliding shorts are a good option for using a cup, as they provide maximum comfort and mobility.

Performance apparel, or form-fitting shirts, shorts, and socks worn under pads and jerseys, are designed to wick sweat away from the body, and also provide some protection from rubbing. Long-sleeved shirts will also protect the arms from turf burns. This apparel also has a high coolness factor, too, especially if it bears good professional lacrosse logos.

Goalie Equipment

Special equipment is required for goalies, including gloves with thicker thumb padding, chest pads, throat protectors, and, at the youth level, hip protectors. Women goalies must wear shin guards and padded pants.

Accessories

Wearing sun-block is always a good idea for players who are outdoors a lot. Keep a tube of sweat-resistant stuff in the gear bag, especially for girls, since they don't have all that padding covering their skin. Wrist bands and head bands come in cool colors and with lacrosse emblems and they keep the inevitable sweat under control. Cool beanies are another accessory popular with lacrosse players, and a way to make their loyalties clear with team colors or emblems.

As you have no doubt realized by now, lacrosse involves a lot of gear. Gear bags help players keep the gear all in one place, rather than taking over your entire house. Girls, because they have less gear, can get by with stick bags, which hold several sticks and have a shoulder strap for easy carrying. These come with compartments for balls and goggles. There are also small backpack type bags for holding goggles and personal items, and some of these have a sleeve for a stick.

Gear bags for boys are mostly of two types: a long, multi-pocket bag with two handles and a shoulder strap, or backpack style bags. Most players want a bag with a compartment for a couple of sticks, a pocket for balls, and plenty of room for helmet, pads and shoes. Some have special compartments for wet gear, or ventilation to keep things from getting too smelly inside. Special bags for the longer defense sticks are available, too.

Throwing a ball against a wall to practice catching is an important drill for lacrosse players. If your house doesn't offer a suitable wall - or you have reached your limit on broken windows - there are freestanding rebound nets that serve the same purpose. Backyard goals allow your player to practice shooting goals at home. There are special training nets intended to simulate a goalie, too, in case dad gets tired of standing in for the goalie while his player practices shots.

Stick tape, used by players to customize the stick grip, comes in a variety of colors.

The Game Bag

Here are the basic contents of a lacrosse player's bag (you can see why it's a big bag!):

a. Stick
b. Gloves
c. Arm pads
d. Shoulder pads
e. Helmet
f. Cleats
g. Balls
h. Water
i. Energy bars
j. Towel
k. Sweatbands
l. Sunscreen
m. First aid kit
n. Spare shirt

    o. Extra socks
    p. Change of clothes
    q. Flip-flops
    r. Money
    s. Paperwork

Fun Stuff

Much of the time, kids just want to have fun. Childhood is short, as any parent of grown children can tell you, so don't be afraid to let them just have fun. Fun products and activities can help your child stay in good physical condition and have a good time, too. For younger kids, and even those who aren't so young, sometimes all it takes to make an activity fun is for you to join in.

Z Ball is a rubber ball covered in knobs that cause it to move in very unpredictable ways. Throwing one of these around - and chasing it - is a fun way to build dexterity and eye-hand coordination. Keep in mind, though, that this fun activity won't completely replace skill work.

A jump rope is fun for all ages, is inexpensive, and doesn't require a special field or court. Jumping rope will improve your child's agility, balance and strength, and give him a great workout, too. Foot speed is one of the fundamentals of lacrosse. Players of all ages, especially bigger defensive players, can benefit from the improved speed that jumping rope helps develop. Get a jump rope that is the right length or one that's adjustable, with padded handles. Pick up a couple, and get in shape with your child.

Shooting trainers such as rebound nets, bounce back targets, "ball walls" of nylon net, goal and corner targets make it easy for players to practice various skills in the comfort and relative obscurity of their own backyard, and with friends and family. Use a ball wall for fun conditioning, but encourage plenty of time on a real concrete or brick wall. Shooting on cages with corner targets is one of the most effective ways to increase shot speed and accuracy. Look for these fun training aids in lacrosse catalogs and websites.

Best Buy

Native Americans enjoyed lacrosse with hand-made sticks and balls and little else. As you have seen from this chapter, though, your child is going to need a bit more equipment than this, and there are enough choices out there to make your head spin. Before you buy something, read about it in this book, in catalogs and on websites, and browse a specialized lacrosse store, if there is one in your area. Ask your kids' coach for advice, too. Just keep in mind the level of play and purpose of a particular piece of equipment when making your selection.

These days, it seems like most of what we buy is influenced by some celebrity or another, perhaps without most of us even realizing it. Youngsters are certainly not immune to the celebrity endorsement and the whole coolness factor of wearing the same thing as someone famous.

It's perfectly fine if you and your player want to check out the equipment and attire of professional lacrosse players. Just be aware that professional's choices are influenced by contracts and endorsement deals. All Major League Lacrosse players, for example, wear Warrior gear because of a contract, not necessarily because it's better equipment.

Warrior gear is great of course, and few athletes would risk injury or poor play with inferior equipment just for a better deal. But that fact, and the fact that many professional players work for one of the lacrosse manufacturing or marketing companies, will influence their choices. Who is wearing what should be just one of many factors you consider when choosing your stuff.

Future Gear

Technology keeps improving in many areas of our lives, and lacrosse gear is no exception. New developments such as offset heads and shafts, lighter and more durable materials such as the plastics for heads and metals for shafts, and better material in glove palms have already been mentioned. No doubt these kinds of improvements will continue.

Take a close look at what a new design or material is intended to do and how important that is to your player, as well as how proven those benefits are, before deciding something is a must-have. The best time to take advantage of new developments is probably when you are upgrading or replacing gear anyway.

Each piece of lacrosse equipment serves a purpose. Protective equipment is required by the rules, which are not, however, always enforced. Leaving out a piece or two of the lacrosse wardrobe - out of laziness, personal preference, a desire to look tough, or any other reason - simply isn't safe. It puts at risk teeth, jaws, ribs, shoulders, hands, heads and other essential body parts. Players won't play better without the necessary equipment. Let the other team make fun; they'll be the ones on the sidelines from injury.

Coaches must set an example, stress the importance of complete equipment, and enforce the rules. Parents must demand that coaches do so. We've simply invested too much in our kids - their teeth, health care, equipment, training, camps and so forth to tolerate unnecessary risk.

Equipment is mainly about safety - a subject near and dear to every parent's heart - and performance, which is near and dear to every player's heart. In fact, the rather impressive gear can be part of the appeal of the sport. What kid doesn't want to slap on armor, even if it is cloth and plastic, and run around with big sticks?

3

Starting Off On The Right Foot

*"Sports encourage discipline, leadership and time management
skills. Equally important, kids get fit and have fun."*
Jordan Metzl, M.D., author of *The Young Athlete*

Now that you discovered more about the game and know
what all that awesome-looking equipment is for, let's talk
about getting your child off on the right lacrosse foot.
Potential lacrosse stars have no doubt been lost to the
sport because their first exposure was with a coach
inexperienced with lacrosse or with coaching in general, or
one not trained to work with the appropriate age group.

Kids who are just trying out the sport sometimes
can end up with a team of more experienced players and
become discouraged when they can't keep up. This can be
a particular problem in cities or towns where lacrosse is
just catching on and more kids come late to the game. It is
tough for a middle or high school kid to be the beginner
among a group of peers who are much farther along with
skills and knowledge.

What it boils down to is this: the first exposure and
early experiences with the sport need to be positive, for
kids of all ages. Otherwise, a kid may not stick with it long
enough to find out whether or not he really likes lacrosse.

The First Coach

Attempting to select the best coach for your child is an
important job for parents. Your options may be limited,
however; as lacrosse is a relatively new sport in many
areas, qualified and experienced coaches can be hard to
find, especially at the youth level. That first coach can be a
big influence on whether or not your child likes and
decides to stay with lacrosse, though.

At the beginner level, good coaching is critical to
learning proper basic skills and techniques. For example,

while lacrosse will always have an element of physical contact, elementary age players should be coached as to the proper checks with the stick only. Some leagues have a two-step checking rule, which means body checks must be within two steps.

At any rate, you will likely find yourself evaluating coaches at several different junctures in your child's lacrosse journey: the first coach, a camp coach, high school level and college. Don't worry so much about the camp director or the head of athletics - although you want leaders who are qualified and knowledgeable. But concentrate on the coach who will be working directly

Questions for a First Coach

1. What is your coaching philosophy - i.e. play to win or play to learn?

2. What coaching experience do you have? It is best if a coach has experience specifically in lacrosse, with children of your child's age.

3. What was your playing experience?

4. Where did you go to school? Ask what level of education the coach completed - generally the higher level completed the better.

5. Do you have first aid and CPR training?

6. What equipment and resources are available for games and practices (e.g. defibrillator)?

7. Does your organization perform background checks on staff?

with your child. There are specific qualifications and attributes to look for.

While there is currently no formal certification for lacrosse coaches, you can look for a coach who has basic training, such as that provided by the Positive Coaching Alliance (More info: positivecoach.org). Experience coaching lacrosse, and specifically experience with youngsters your child's age, is a must. Too many football coaches have run off potential lacrosse players. Look at a coach's playing history and experience and find out if his or her general philosophy about the game, youth sports and competition are in line with yours. Then keep an eye on what the players are being taught about the sport. If you have questions about something the coach is doing, ask.

The first goal of the coach of young players, according to Tal Alter, former development associate at Positive Coaching Alliance, should be to work on developing the team culture as one where players feel privileged to be part of the team and want to help their teammates succeed.

"It's not a coincidence that good teams always seem to have good chemistry," Alter says, "More often than not, good chemistry stems from a strong team culture, which develops as a result of a healthy coaching philosophy."

Coaches make that team culture happen by clearly and consistently articulating to their players a philosophy that emphasizes high standards for effort and attitude, and allows for mistakes to be okay.

Make sure that teaching good sportsmanship is an important part of the coach's game plan. Learning how to win and lose with class is a lesson that your child will put to use in future life experiences.

Making it Fun

Whatever else you do, remember that the key is FUN. After all, lacrosse is a game. The ability to make lacrosse fun - at practice, games and in between - is the most important qualification for your child's first coach. In a choice between a top-level, world famous coach who is always frowning, or a lesser-known coach who emphasizes fun and the love of the game, go for the second guy every time. If your kid is having a good time, he will be motivated to continue working on the game.

Look at the way a coach teaches - that fun aspect again - but also at his or her attitude. A coach should be enthusiastic; someone who rewards effort as much as achievement, creates an environment that encourages kids to try new skills, and who can focus on each child even in a group situation. The best way to assess all this is to watch a coach in action over the course of several practices or camp sessions. Take your child with you. The time spent on this will be well worth it, because, again, that first coach will play a big role in whether or not your child becomes a lacrosse player.

Parent as Coach

You're a concerned, involved parent, or you wouldn't be reading this book. But parenting your children and coaching them are two completely different animals, each with its own challenges and rewards. Think hard before trying to do both.

A parent who was a college or professional level lacrosse player will naturally want to pass on some of the wisdom and ability gained from that play to his or her child. That may be possible when your kids are younger and while the play is mostly recreational. In fact, without parents volunteering as coaches, leagues at this level would have a hard time making teams. But once a child enters the teen years, or becomes more serious about the game, being his or her coach can be a real challenge. Emotions can get in the way, causing problems between parent and child as well as coach and child.

It is in your child's best interest to limit any coaching by you the parent to those earlier years. After that, you can continue to play with your child, as long as you focus on that key word - play. Remember that you are enjoying time with your child and the game itself, rather than teaching or coaching. If your child has questions, feel free to provide them guidance based on your knowledge and philosophy. Parents can be the best teachers of positive sportsmanship by helping their youngsters keep in perspective that it is always just a game. Keep in mind that youngsters play sports for fun, and learning is a natural consequence.

If you never picked up a lacrosse stick in your life, or don't have the slightest interest in coaching your child, you should still be involved in those early years. Be willing to toss the ball around. Those of us with less-than-impressive reflexes may find that a baseball glove works well for catching lacrosse balls tossed from our child's stick. Make a game attempt at joining him in wall ball, and be an enthusiastic spectator at games and camps.

Children need to experience an emotional involvement if they are going to choose lacrosse as their sport. As a parent, you are most qualified to offer your child memorable lacrosse experiences. Even - or perhaps especially - if those memories are of dad catching the ball with his face more often than the stick, or of mom breaking yet another window. Don't be the parent who beats up another parent over a loss, or berates the officials over a call. Be positive and supportive of effort and enthusiasm, and help everyone remember the game is about fun.

The Right Age

Most of today's college and professional lacrosse players started the sport in middle or high school. The sport is becoming more mainstream and growing rapidly, though, and more and more players will start at younger ages.

Jumpstart Interest

It is just plain common sense that a youngster needs basic comprehension of instructions, command of the language, and motor skills before considering any sport. That sets the bottom limit at about three years of age. That doesn't mean all kids are ready to start sports at age three, by any means, any more than they are ready to get married at age 18 just because it's legal. Three-year-olds have short attention spans, lack the cognitive skills to grasp the concept of teamwork, and don't have a lot of physical strength. Most of them would rather roll balls around on the ground than catch them. So don't get carried away.

Introduce your child to sports in a general, fun way, by watching sports together - especially actual games, versus televised ones - and playing some simple games like catch and even tag. Most kids will enjoy these activities simply because you are doing something with them, so capitalize on that. Pay attention to what she seems to enjoy and be most interested in, and expand on it. If he looks forward to tossing a ball back and forth, make yourself available to do that pretty much as often as he wants to. If the interest isn't there yet, back off and try again in six months or a year. Take your cues from your child.

Kids who participate early in athletic activities of all kinds will develop good physical fitness and all-around athletic abilities. Sports, team sports in particular, have a lot to teach children – positive things like cooperation, teamwork, self-improvement, good sportsmanship, perseverance, leadership and confidence. Kids also get important and needed exercise while they're at it, although parents don't have to tell them that. In fact, kids who play sports are developing fitness habits that will contribute to their overall health for life - especially important these days when weight problems are a national epidemic.

Perhaps most important, kids can have a lot of fun playing sports, and parents should put the emphasis on that fun, and keep the competition in perspective. Be sure your children also have plenty of time for other interests, including family time, social pursuits and school. One successful coach suggests putting family first, school second, and sports third.

Participation in Other Sports

It is important to encourage your youngsters to play a variety of sports, rather than "specializing" in one. Focusing too intently on any one sport at a young age can have negative consequences. While your young athlete may see himself playing just one sport if he is good at that sport, Kevin Anderson, assistant lacrosse coach at Notre Dame, cautions that he may miss out on valuable skills and lessons by forgoing other sports.

Youngsters have many choices of sports to play today - soccer, tennis, baseball, basketball, swimming, lacrosse and many more. Help your kids find several different ones to play while they are young. According to Bob Bigelow, a former NBA professional basketball player and author of *Just Let the Kids Play*, playing games of all types teaches kids a variety of skills that will serve them well when it is time for "serious" play. Specialization should wait until at least age 15 or 16.

There are several good reasons for this. For one thing, it is difficult, if not impossible, to tell your child's true physical talents until after puberty. Bigelow didn't play organized basketball until high school and, in fact, admits he wasn't very good at all at age ten. When basketball superstar Michael Jordan tried out for the varsity squad as a high school sophomore, he was cut. That summer, Jordan grew six inches.

For another thing, specialization in one sport at an early age can have serious physical consequences. Repetitive-use injuries like stress fractures, growth plate disorders, cracked kneecaps, frayed heel tendons and back problems - previously only seen in adults - are reaching epidemic proportions in young teens as kids play one sport year-round and focus on single skills like kicking or throwing. Those young, growing bodies just can't take it - not that older, full-grown ones can, either.

The American Academy of Pediatrics went so far as to issue a formal statement warning of the risks of repetitive injury for children who practice one sport year-round or at the "elite" level. The statement said, in part,

"Those who participate in a variety of sports and specialize only after reaching puberty tend to be more consistent performers, have fewer injuries, and adhere to sports play longer than those who specialize early."

The American Academy of Orthopedic Surgeons weighed in, too, with a public service campaign that asks "Which will they have longer, their trophies or their injuries?" Overuse injuries can cause permanent damage and contribute to diseases later in life, such as osteoarthritis.

According to Jordan Metzl, M.D., author of *The Young Athlete: A Sports Doctor's Complete Guide for Parents*, this is partly due to kids playing competitive sports at younger ages. Kids run twice the risk of being injured when playing organized sports. As parents, few of us would think that an injury that will hinder our child for life is a reasonable price to pay for a winning season in any sport. Keep the long-term perspective in mind.

Specialization isn't even the best way to develop your child's full potential. "I believe that all athletes should try to play multiple sports as long as they can," says Notre Dame's Anderson. "There are so many valuable skills, lessons and characteristics an athlete can learn and develop by playing a variety of sports." Not only that, but playing other sports can actually improve your kid's lacrosse game.

A former Brown University player and current lacrosse league president points out that basketball and football are great cross-training for lacrosse - the former teaches movement away from the ball, and football is good for building agility.

It's also important to recognize that kids won't acquire skills faster just because they start a sport younger. In fact, getting too serious about a sport at a young age can even cause kids to burn out and quit altogether. According to Fred Engh, author of *Why Johnny Hates Sports*, 70 percent of all youngsters drop out of organized sports by age 13 because of unpleasant experiences. You probably don't want your child to be in that 70 percent.

All that said, lacrosse is a great sport for kids, and if your child gets interested in it at a young age, by all means let the kid play on a league team in the spring season and attend a summer camp and maybe play on a recreational holiday league in the winter. Just allow - and even encourage - your young child to hang out with friends and spend plenty of time in unstructured play.

Go ahead and sign up for the football or volleyball team in the fall and maybe throw in a basketball or soccer camp, too. If your child really likes lacrosse, continue to let him play during season, attend camps in summer and take advantage of other opportunities to enjoy the sport. Just remember that playing other sports, too, will make him a better lacrosse player in the long run.

Ultimately, the question is not "What is the right age for my child to start playing lacrosse?" It is, "What is the best way to get my child started in sports in general, and lacrosse in particular, taking into account his or her age and needs?"

Goal Setting

Although kids can start lacrosse at almost any age, the age at which your child starts playing will play a part in the goals she should have for the future. Make sure those goals are realistic. A player who picks up the game at age 18 may still play college lacrosse, but perhaps not Division I. If he is generally athletic and really loves the game, he can probably find a team to play on and even get onto a college team.

Many colleges are just now forming club lacrosse teams, creating opportunities for players. If your youngster starts in middle school and has the right athletic tools, she has a reasonable shot at a Division I or Division II college team, if the desire is there. Remember, though, that more and more kids are starting every year, and with more players comes more competition at the top levels. While ten years ago, a line three midfielder from Baltimore or Long Island was a potential recruit, these days, only the top athletes and most skilled players are competing for Division I spots.

The bottom line is that kids can pick up lacrosse at any age. They'll just need goals that are in line with that starting age. The learning curve for the game is short, and beginning players usually pick up the basics fairly quickly. After that, it takes a bit longer and a fair amount of practice to master the game.

Kids who were active and exposed to team sports in elementary school, have participated in a wide variety of sports, and are generally athletic can become excellent lacrosse players even if they never picked up a stick before senior year of high school.

For every age there is a right way to introduce this or any sport. For very young kids, say kindergarten and first grade, sports should be sized appropriately, such as with smaller fields or softer balls. Lacrosse has modified rules and may use smaller fields for younger ages. Coaching of kids this age should emphasize effort and good sportsmanship, and above all, having fun.

Teamwork is pretty much a concept too advanced for kids at this age. You just want young kids to be active and moving - and enjoying it. Skill development - and caring about winning and losing - can wait. They'll be developing eye-hand coordination, balance and speed naturally as they grow and play.

For older elementary school age kids, the emphasis can shift a little to teamwork and basic game strategy, still with a focus on everyone playing and enjoying the game. At this age, and older, lacrosse camps are a fun way to introduce the sport or build skill. A camp involves a commitment of only a week or two, versus a season, and typically there is less emphasis on serious competition and more on individual skills and fun. Recreational leagues are fine for this age, too.

The Right Team

Positive early experiences for your child can lead to a long involvement with lacrosse, while negative ones can mean a potential player lost to the sport. Spend some time looking for camps and teams right for your child, places where he will fit comfortably in terms of ability and experience, where the coach knows lacrosse and knows kids of this age, and where the philosophy is on creating players who love the game - and giving everyone equal playing time - not on toting up impressive statistics.

First Instruction

Private instruction is big in many sports, but perhaps not so much in lacrosse. It is available in some areas, and it can be a good way for a player to develop basic skills before joining a team. It may be most appropriate for more advanced players as a way to hone specific skills and advance the level of ability.

For group instruction, initial classes should have only first-timers of roughly the same age. However, just because kids are the same age doesn't mean they should be in class together. Ability is more important than age at this point, although your six-year-old beginner shouldn't be in the same group with thirteen year-olds. A private coach should be able to work with each player, and kids should leave feeling as if they have accomplished something.

Private Lessons
Private lessons can cost anywhere from $30 to $80 per hour, which may be a good investment for a youngster who wants to pick up basics in a hurry in order to join a team. Learning skills the right way early on will pay off in the long run.

A player who got off on the wrong foot and developed bad habits can benefit from private instruction, too. It's a good idea to have an initial coach-parent conference to discuss training objectives and the coach's philosophy. You should continue to have these on a regular basis. Lessons will typically be an hour long and, at least at first, one-on-one. Sessions should stress the basics, like throwing, catching, and switching hands.

A private lesson can be a good place to work on switching hands, one of the basic but more difficult skills of lacrosse. A youngster won't have to worry about being clumsy with the non-dominant hand when no one but the instructor is looking. After half-a-dozen sessions or so, the coach may have two or three kids take instruction together. This will, in fact, be a good thing for players, as they can learn what they are doing right or wrong by watching each other.

Many coaches will offer private lessons, but you may want to consider someone outside of your program to expose your child to a different role model/coach and their skills and philosophies.

Camps
Lacrosse camps are becoming more common around the country, and are a great way to introduce kids to the sport. Look for a camp that welcomes, and nurtures, beginners and that has a philosophy in line with yours. At a camp, a ratio of one coach to fifteen players is ideal, with one to

twenty at the most, for middle schoolers and up. For the younger kids, the ratio should be one coach to ten players.

Find a camp in your area, or one that suits your child's needs and preferences, by talking to your coach, visiting the local lacrosse store, and looking for notices in local youth publications. Call sports offices or check websites to find camps affiliated with universities, such as the University of Denver and Johns Hopkins in Baltimore (More info: lacrossecamps.com and uslaxcamps.com).

Recreational leagues are also becoming more common, and can be a good place to start, as long as kids are generally in the same place in terms of experience with the game. In other words, you don't want to put your brand-new-to-lacrosse child on a team with a bunch of kids who have been playing for a couple of years.

Recreational teams should have no more than 20 to 25 players, and should have a stated policy of giving everyone adequate playing time. Check with a lacrosse store or check lacrosse and city websites, or ask other parents, to find leagues in your area.

Decide the best way for your kid to get started, depending on age, ability and other factors. Then get out there, have fun, and support your player for as long and as far as he or she wants to go in lacrosse. You'll be creating memories to treasure for years to come.

4

Developing Lacrosse Stars

*"I look for a player who is defined not by his natural abilities,
but by the work ethic, natural leadership and competitive spirit.
The only way a player will reach the full potential of his natural
ability, and exceed it, is with the attitude to achieve and
compete."*
Alex Cade, Coronado High School head coach, San
Francisco Dragons goalie

Games are what it's all about for a lacrosse player, but
plenty goes on in between games, too. Team practices and
individual skill work and conditioning are important
activities that determine how well a player and his or her
team will do - and how much fun games will be.

Parents play an important role in setting the tone,
encouraging regular skill work and conditioning, and
keeping   everyone   focused   on   fun   and   good
sportsmanship. This chapter gives you direction about
what your player can expect from team practices, and the
things players can do on their own to improve their skills
and game.

Good Practices

Practice with teammates is very important in a team sport
like lacrosse. Kids need to be practicing with other players
of their age and ability - ideally, their teammates if they
are on a team. Parents can, and should, play catch and
other games with their child, but real practice should be
left to the coach and team. Consider yourself your child's
ready-and-willing   catch   partner   and   all-around
cheerleader, not his or her coach.

If you have a question about or disagreement with
something a coach tells your child, don't contradict the
coach in front of your child. Speak with him about it
privately. A good rule of thumb might be to believe about

half of what your child tells you about the coach, and hope that the coach will believe about half of what your kid tells him about you.

Lacrosse coaches, whether private or team, aren't going to want parents on the field. They will, however, welcome your help off the field. And remember, while the coach is teaching your child lacrosse skills, you are the main teacher when it comes to things such as attitude, character and life skills.

For younger kids, practices should be low-key with a big emphasis on fun. Kids can learn a lot of skills and strategies by playing various fun and instructive games, such as sharks and minnows. But be sure coaches combine these games with actual lacrosse game play right away.

Most lacrosse players will tell you the fun of the game is why they play, and the sooner kids get to experience that, the better. That doesn't mean they need to be playing serious, full-length games right away. But a real scrimmage the first day - with other players of the same level and ability - will get most kids hooked. After all, most kids are at a class or on a team not to *learn* lacrosse but to *play* it. The coach should, of course, discuss the rules before this first scrimmage, so kids know what is and isn't allowed.

A fun, effective team practice will include these elements:

✓ stretching/warm-up
✓ skill work
✓ team work, and
✓ some kind of game or simulation of a game.

The skill work can include other games like sharks and minnows or wall ball. Some other familiar games that can be used in practice are explained below.

Line Drill

Players form two lines, one player behind another, the players at the front of the lines facing each other with twenty yards or more between them. The front player of one line throws the ball to the player at the front of the other line then runs to the back of the line receiving his pass. The player on the other line catches the ball, then throws it back to the first line and runs to the end of the opposite line.

The throws should mix up ground balls, right-handed passes, left-handed passes, over-the-shoulder throws and so forth. Line drills have been a staple of warm-up at practices for years and should be part of every warm-up, just not all of it. Coaches have also found various other drills that focus on stick work, and changing up a drill keeps players on their feet and engaged.

Two on One Ground Balls

This game teaches basic skills and communication on the field. Three players stand or lie on the ground next to the coach, who rolls a ground ball out. Two players are on the same "team" and work against the other player to get the ground ball, using communication and team work. The lone player is learning hustle and overcoming greater odds. Players love this drill and it really breaks down important skills of the game.

Any games used should simulate basic techniques needed to operate efficiently and effectively in a game. As much as possible, games should involve using skills - whether catching, throwing, or something else - at full speed, or the way the skill would be employed in a game situation.

The coach can use game-like drills to identify and correct player errors. Coaches can also ask questions about what a player should be thinking and anticipating in the games, teaching them technique and problem-solving. Always, though, the emphasis is on having fun.

Once a Week

You'll probably want to start with lessons or practices once a week. In the early stages, less is more. If your player is loving lacrosse and clamors for more practices or lessons, consider mixing it up. If he is on a team, add a private lesson, or encourage him to get together with some of his teammates to play wall ball or a pick-up game.

In fact, wall ball ought to be a daily activity for a lacrosse player; short periods, say ten minutes, for young players, and longer ones, fifteen or twenty, for middle and high school age kids. If your player loves wall ball, the sky is the limit, though. Kids who want to just can't spend too much time on this. Experienced players say it makes their game more versatile and makes them consistent and reliable when handling the ball.

Finding a Wall

So your kid is all excited about lacrosse and in between weekly practices can't wait to have some fun with you and a ball and stick. In a perfect world, you'd be just as good at catching and throwing as your child is, and have as much time to play. But that probably isn't the case. Tossing the ball back and forth is a fine activity, but remember that your kid should be practicing skills at full speed. Chances are, your youngster can catch and throw a bit faster than you. So he needs that daily dose of wall ball.

Maybe you are lucky and have a two-story brick wall on your house with no windows at risk. Or maybe not. Fortunately, good walls aren't that hard to find. Just follow a few basic rules when picking one to use. If it is a private building, ask permission. You probably don't need to ask permission to use the neighborhood school gym wall, or the backboard of the school tennis courts.

Just use some common sense. If there are windows nearby, the wall probably isn't a good choice. If there are cars parked either behind the backboard or wall, or close behind the player, you should probably pass on that one, too. And it should go without saying that wherever your kid plays wall ball, he will be sure not to leave any trash behind or trample any landscaping.

If you have access to a racquetball court, these make excellent places to play wall ball. The surface is smooth and so returns the ball accurately, and the enclosed space means no chasing missed balls down the block.

If you just can't find a suitable wall nearby, you can buy portable rebounding walls from lacrosse suppliers. There are several online suppliers that sell rebound nets that retail for from $200 to $250.

Getting in Shape

Getting in shape for a game in any sport involves conditioning of both the body and mind. Players must stay in shape through continuous effort, which is a great habit for lifelong fitness.

Physical Conditioning

Athletes who are in good physical shape will not only play better and not tire out during a game, they are also less likely to get injured. A lacrosse player, depending on the position played, is likely to run up and down the field as many as 40 times during a game - the equivalent of running anywhere from four to eight miles.

While doing that, the player also has to concentrate on stick work, hold onto the ball or attempt to get it from another player, look for open players, and note where defenders are. Less effort expended on the actual running means more available for everything else. In short, good lacrosse players need to be in great shape!

Coaches of younger players won't want to spend much of their kids' valuable practice time on physical fitness. Instead, your kid should establish a regular workout regimen between practices. Younger players can aim for running some, and playing in the backyard with friends is likely to be sufficient. Older players should regularly run a few miles a week for endurance, with some interval training mixed in. Beginning players should be able to achieve this basic level of fitness in three months of work.

Core fitness and flexibility are important too. Kids can start strength training with light weights around adolescence, when growth plates on the bones have begun to close. Any strength-training program your child participates in should be run by a skilled professional, such as a physical therapist or certified trainer, because improper technique can lead to injury. Another way to achieve core fitness and flexibility is working with exercise balls, which can be a lot of fun. Strongly encourage a brisk warm-up followed by ten minutes of stretching before any physical activity.

Allow young kids to engage in normal kid activities like climbing trees or swinging, too; they'll be building muscle and bone density and not even know it. Formal flexibility training such as yoga is good, and is something that can be done at home once kids understand the basics. Yoga can also improve agility and the mind-body connection. It isn't a bad activity for parents, either.

Lacrosse players should also work on forearm strength, which is necessary for gripping the stick. This can be done as part of weight work-outs, or through push-ups and other upper-body exercises.

A balanced conditioning program will include training for flexibility, strength, power, speed, agility, quickness and cardiovascular fitness. Incorporating all these elements can be challenging. Mixing up various activities is important, and always include warm-up.

Get the blood flowing, perhaps by taking a lap around the track, followed by stretching exercises. These should be done the same way each time, starting with the back and legs, then abdomen/groin, head and shoulders. Then players can toss a ball back and forth or take some shots at the goal. Warming up can be done before practice or as it gets started.

Interval training

Most lacrosse positions require constant bursts of high energy during a game. During these bursts, the body uses energy stored in the muscles in the form of glycogen and an energy byproduct called ATP, short for adenosine triphosphate. The by-product of metabolizing this energy is lactic acid, which is responsible for the burning sensation athletes feel in their muscles during a strenuous workout. During periods of normal activity, the body works to break down the lactic acid built up during the workout.

Interval training helps develop the body for this kind of activity and develops muscles with higher tolerance of lactic acid build-up. At normal levels of activity, the body uses oxygen to convert stored carbohydrates into energy. With interval training, the body builds new capillaries and is better able to deliver oxygen to working muscles. This results in increased performance for an athlete.

To interval train, kids start with a gradual warm-up, then start running at about 70 percent of maximum speed, which is just under a full sprint. After about one minute, they slow down to normal running speed for two minutes, then increase back to 70 percent for another minute. Run at a relaxed pace for five minutes to cool down.

In addition to running sprints like this, playing Frisbee in the park is good interval training. The technique can also be used with cycling, skating or swimming. Kids who don't like watching the clock can use laps around the track, spaces between street lights or some other marker instead.

Plyometrics

An athlete's ability to increase speed of movement and improve power production, or the ability to "explode," is enhanced with plyometrics training. These exercises involve rapid stretch followed by rapid shortening of a muscle. Lunges with weights or standing broad jumps repeated for short but intense time periods will build muscle fibers that will start to train the body to react more quickly.

Always start by warming up the muscles completely. Ask your coach or local gym about Plyometrics drills designed for kids using soft cones, medicine balls and other equipment. Common kid activities like skipping, hopscotch, jumping jacks and some aerobic dance moves are forms of Plyometrics.

Regular Exercise

Parents can help make exercise fun for kids in a variety of ways. Most importantly, look at it as an enjoyable activity that your child can look forward to for its own sake, rather than a chore or means to an end. If possible, make it a family activity.

Take your child to the local hike and bike trail on pretty days. Supply a favorite flavor of sport drink after a run, and an occasional healthy treat like frozen yogurt. Fun t-shirts and funky socks (especially for girls) just for running can make suiting up more appealing.

Mix it up - instead of running, ride bikes once a week, or skip rope. Go swimming or skating. Walk the dog. Avoid too much structure at younger ages - kids can just play and be active rather than do formal exercise, which can start to seem like work if you're not careful. Kids will follow your example, parents. Stay fit and active, and they will, too.

For older kids who like tangible goals, have them keep a log and reward a certain number of miles run with a cool lacrosse t-shirt or shorts. Or, let kids set a goal to improve their running time by so much, and reward that accomplishment. Remember, pushing the body to run a little farther or a little faster is a good mental toughness exercise.

Mental Conditioning

Speaking of mental toughness, athletes must condition the mind as well as the body. Mental conditioning incorporated into routines like lacrosse practice can develop not only a better player but a better person.

Mental fitness includes three components: mental attitude, emotional toughness, and mind-body coordination. Attitude is nurtured by both coaches, on the field, and parents, off of it. Emotional toughness and mind-body coordination develop naturally in practices, but can be boosted with martial arts or yoga training.

Parents can play a big role as their child's mental coach. This doesn't have to be complicated or time-consuming. Insisting that a player shake hands with members of the opposing team after a game sends a positive message. After a game, parents can ask "how did the team play?" or "did you have a good time?" rather than "who won?" as part of a general de-emphasis on wins and losses.

The post-game handshake ritual also reinforces the idea of respect for opponents and good sportsmanship. Choose appropriate times to talk about the mental aspects of the game with your kid, preferably during non-lacrosse activities. It's okay to reinforce those talks with gentle reminders on the way to practice or a game. Here are some questions to stimulate the discussion:

- What is the true nature of competition? Is it a threat or challenge? Can it help you improve your game? Become a better person?
- Is your child afraid of competition? What can she do to stay relaxed and enjoy the challenge?
- When kids face off against good friends, can they reconcile not wanting to hurt a friend's feelings and wanting to win?
- At what level of play are skill development and effort more important than the result of the game?
- Do you compete to please yourself, your parents, your coach, or all of the above? Why is playing for your own enjoyment important?

Keep in mind the other influences on your child's mental conditioning. Big ones are television shows and movies. These may emphasize winning at all costs, which can send a message counter to yours. It helps to set good television habits. Restrict the amount of time kids watch, especially younger ones, and don't be afraid to set some boundaries about what types of shows they are allowed to watch. Find shows with positive messages and watch them together. Even shows with less-than-stellar messages can be useful if you watch with your child (or with older kids, at least see the same movies) and discuss what you're seeing.

Playing a Variety of Sports

Participation in other sports is a good way to develop and maintain physical and mental conditioning. Sports that complement lacrosse well include hockey, basketball, football and soccer. In fact, the only sports that wouldn't enhance a lacrosse player's performance are those that are played during the same season and conflict with lacrosse involvement.

Some parents try to have their children playing lacrosse as well as baseball or track and field. It may work at younger ages as long as the child participates because he wants to and as long as it is fun. In middle or high school, it becomes more difficult to do as academic rigor increases. But participation in other sports during other seasons, and exercising outside of lacrosse, are good ways to strengthen different muscle groups, and reduce the risk of overuse injury.

Academic Achievement

If you need another reason to love lacrosse, consider this: studies have proven that physical fitness contributes to academic achievement. In a study by the California Department of Education, students with high scores in fitness also scored high in reading and math. Those who met minimum fitness levels in three or more of six physical fitness areas showed the greatest gains in academic achievement in all three grade levels studied.

The study used a physical fitness test known as the Fitnessgram (More info: cooperinst.org) to assess cardiovascular endurance, percentage of body fat, abdominal strength and endurance, trunk strength and flexibility, upper body strength and endurance, and overall flexibility. Reading and math levels were tested using the Stanford Achievement Test, part of California's Standardized Testing and Reporting Program.

Healthful Habits

Good healthy habits are as important as conditioning, if not more so. Kids need to eat a well-balanced diet, stay hydrated, and get plenty of rest. A regular sleep schedule, with an hour or less variation from a regular bedtime and wake time, promotes better sleep and body rhythms. Young bodies especially need rest when muscles are sore; rest is when the muscles grow. Athletes who don't get adequate rest are more likely to get injured. Most coaches will encourage players to take it easy the day before a game.

Competition requires even more attention to good nutrition. Eating the right foods the day before and day of a game will keep a player's energy level high. Foods rich in carbohydrates are good body fuel - whole-grain breads, potatoes and pasta, pancakes, bagels, raisins and bananas are some. Athletes need to have plenty of protein in their diet as well - foods such as nuts (including peanut butter), cheese, and eggs. It is important to refuel several hours after a game as well.

Regular hydration is extremely important, and while sports beverages are fine, most contain added sugar and other ingredients young bodies don't really need. Plain old water is best. Athletes should, in general, avoid drinks containing high amounts of sugar. A number of studies show that high-calorie soft drinks are a cause of increased weight in youngsters. A study in the March, 2006 issue of *Pediatrics* showed that cutting back on sugary drinks reduced body fat in teens. Liquid calories tend to increase overall calorie intake - they don't fill kids up, don't change what they eat, and don't provide nutrition.

Unfortunately, sodas have become a daily habit for most teens, and at the same time, their consumption of milk, an important source of calcium, has decreased. Parents can help by stocking the refrigerator with pitchers of cold water instead of sodas, and encouraging kids to make other choices when away from home.

One family encouraged the kids to stick with water at restaurants by putting the $1 or $2 that each soda would have cost into a jar and using the money for special treats like a movie or another meal out - with water to drink, of course. Nutritionists recommend that kids make water their first choice, followed by unsweetened tea or coffee, and low-fat or nonfat milk - with sodas far down the list.

Multivitamins with antioxidants and minerals are good for young bodies. Parents should be cautious about other dietary supplements, even "natural" ones like herbs. Research the supplement and check with your child's doctor before having your child take them. Be aware that there are sometimes interactions between supplements and other medications. Also, because these dietary supplements are not regulated the way medicines are, check labels carefully to see what a particular product contains and in what amounts. Some that are labeled for a particular ingredient may actually have very little of that substance in them.

Steroid supplements should be avoided. College lacrosse players are tested for recreational drugs and steroids at tournaments and possibly other times.

Avoiding Burnout

Unpleasant experiences cause 70 percent of all youngsters to drop out of organized sports by age 13. It doesn't have to be one extremely unpleasant occurrence - many small unpleasant ones can add up to burnout.

One of the primary ways to avoid burnout in young lacrosse players is to manage the type and number of experiences, such as camps and off-season games. It is also important to reward effort and de-emphasize results during a young player's development phase. Kids need to experience success in terms of personal improvement and team wins, but too much winning leads to boredom. Kids need to be challenged - their play will not improve unless they compete against the best teams. Parents can monitor their player and be sure that he is experiencing that success but also getting challenged enough - and if not, adjust things accordingly.

Developing other interests also helps avoid burnout. Again, encourage your kids to participate in different sports for recreation, and be sure they engage in other activities - computers, music, family outings - as well.

Burnout often kicks in when kids hit the teen years. Younger kids generally go along with whatever their parents have planned for them. But around adolescence kids begin to assert themselves more and more. In addition, by this time years of competition and over-scheduling may have taken their toll. Watch for signs so you can detect burnout early and make needed changes before it's too late.

A child who asks to miss practice or complains about the coach or team may be telling you he has problems. Kids suffering burnout may show signs of sleep disturbance, headache or muscle rigidity, even signs of depression. If you think you are dealing with burnout, cut back on both lacrosse and other extra-curricular activities. Kids who have been exclusively into lacrosse can be encouraged to participate in a new activity. Make this change in a positive way; rather than pointing out that there seems to be a problem and a change needs to be made, present it as a new opportunity. Give your child several options and let him choose.

Have a Higher Goal

Coaches should emphasize that family and school come before lacrosse. While players must make a commitment to their team, they also should know that if the family has an event or emergency, they may have to miss a practice or even a game - and that is okay. Players should take care of academic obligations in order to be eligible to participate in lacrosse. If a player is not keeping up in the classroom, sports may have to be put on hold for a while. Setting priorities will actually ease the pressure on your child and allow her to be more relaxed.

Good Pain, Bad Pain

A little discomfort is a normal part of sports and conditioning. Making muscles stronger requires pushing them beyond normal limits, resulting in that "burn" and, ultimately, fatigue. This is good pain. It should be short-lived and go away in a matter of hours with rest.

Some pain lasts longer, and affects sports performance along with other functions such as sleep, walking, or getting dressed. Pain like this, or pain that doesn't go away after rest, is bad pain. Talk to your kids about the difference, and always treat bad pain with concern and medical attention. Never allow your child to play through pain. Potential lifelong impairment simply isn't worth it.

Kids may not always be completely honest about their pain, especially if a big game is coming up and they really want to play in it. The best way to avoid this scenario is to talk to your kids about pain and injuries early on, before any occur. Explain the difference between good and bad pain, and the importance of taking care of bad pain and injuries in a timely manner. Most kids will be able to see the down side of playing in that big game with an injury that could lead to being sidelined for the season or, rarely, for good. Concussions, for example, need to be taken seriously, and players should seek medical attention for a suspected concussion.

Pains common to lacrosse will include sore leg muscles from running, sore arm muscles from stick work, sore heels, sore shins - called shin splints - and possibly some bruises. Proper conditioning will minimize soreness and help avoid injury. Good nutrition and hydration will also help, as will an adequate warm-up and stretching before and after the game. Check the fit and condition of protective equipment on occasion, too.

Other healthy habits that will help your child avoid injury include proper equipment, especially shoes appropriate for the playing surface and that fit well. Be sure all your player's gear fits well. Kids who are going through growth spurts can experience heel pain after running in cleats. Solve the problem with gel heel inserts in the shoes, ice (a bag of frozen peas works well as it molds to fit the heel), or ibuprofen before and after practice.

Getting in healthy shape and practicing regularly - individually and with the team - is enjoyable for kids. Having fun in between games will keep them coming back for more, too. The encouragement and support of parents is important in player development - and it isn't bad for the parents, either.

5

Turning Up The Heat

"Lacrosse players are made, not born."
Scott Hochstadt, three time All-American, University of Maryland

Winning is not everything. But in sports, it is certainly important. It becomes more so as children get older.

With very young players, sports are all about fun and games. When kids get a little older, many are involved in sports because they enjoy being part of something and hanging out with their friends. Heading into adolescence, additional motivation comes from competition and the desire to win.

Just how important competition is to an individual player depends partly on personality and partly on factors such as the role models they have and the family values they've been immersed in. Parents just need to remember to keep enjoyment of the game the top priority, even when the competition heats up. Sometimes, however, the enjoyment actually comes from being part of a winning program or one with a rich history. This can teach your child two parts of the persona he may not have known existed - heart and pride.

Kids have a natural desire to compete and to win, and that is good. Teenage lacrosse players who win more games than they lose are more likely to want to continue playing and working to become better.

Accept your child's natural desire to win, but don't emphasize winning or push for wins at all cost. One of the reasons competition gets a bad rap is because children are pushed into too much of it before they are ready.

Learning to Win

"Winners don't just let it happen, they make it happen," says Scott Hochstadt, a three-time All American at the University of Maryland who played professional lacrosse in both the indoor and outdoor leagues. "You need to work on the little things to make yourself a lacrosse player."

Winners give their all not just during games, but also in practice and other preparation for those games. All great players understand that you can't just show up for a game and expect to win. You need to prepare yourself by practicing hard, taking care of your body, and understanding the mental aspect of the game. Every athlete should have the goal of achieving peak physical condition before and maintaining it throughout every season.

Raising the Bar

When the competition is too easy, it devalues a player's accomplishments. Ask any college or professional player about the wins that have meant the most and you'll hear about the tough game against a talented and competitive opponent that was hard-fought and hard-won. You probably won't hear about the thrashing of a clearly less-talented team, because it just didn't mean as much.

While it is important for kids to win, at some point, a player needs better competition to progress. Kids who play against the best will reach higher levels. This is part of the reason most US lacrosse college coaches still have an East Coast bias, for example. A great player may come out of California, but that player has not competed against the best and been truly tested.

Parents, as well as coaches, play an important role in keeping the focus on the positive aspects of competition. Parents also should be gauging when their kids are ready for tougher competition and when it might be too much. Mental maturity is as important, if not more important, than physical development here.

This is a subjective decision and no one knows your kid better than you do. A kid who seems bored or finds practices and games too easy may be ready for a higher level of competition. Some kids thrive on and even need a little pressure to help them perform up to their potential, while others wither under pressure. Either way, things may be too tough if your child seems constantly frustrated (occasional frustration is okay) or stressed.

Signs of stress vary from one kid to another, but may include change in sleep habits, seeming withdrawn or quiet (especially if this is not a kid's natural personality), falling grades, or acting out. Kids who talk about not having fun anymore or say they want to quit may be competing at a level higher than what they are ready for.

Parents who have good communication with their kids will be better able to gauge what is best for them. Open communication between you and your child is something that starts early and never stops. This is how you really get to know your child.

Talk often, about lacrosse as well as other things going on in your kid's life, and really listen to him. Ask how things are going - and keep asking through the teen years, when a grunt may be your only answer. Kids want to know that you are genuinely interested in what is going on with them, even when they won't admit it. When you ask, keep an open mind, and be prepared for answers you may not want to hear.

The idea is to make lacrosse challenging enough to inspire your kid to try harder and develop as a player, without discouraging or humiliating her, or asking too much of your youngster too soon. Parents can run children away from sports by trying to make them into something they are not. Let your child ultimately be the one who chooses to play for the advanced team.

Determining Readiness

Both a child's maturity and his or her competency in the sport must be considered in determining what level of competition is appropriate. Parents may be the best judge of their child's maturity, but generally children eight years old and younger are not ready to handle rigorous competition in any sport. Between ages eight and ten, they can be eased into it. During this time, you should be teaching them about winning and losing. Once your child is mentally ready, probably around age 13, confer with the coach about his or her competency.

Becoming Aggressive on the Field

A player can be the nicest kid in town off the field, and players should always display good sportsmanship. But consistently winning games requires aggressiveness on the field. This isn't the same thing as being obnoxious, talking trash, or acting like a jerk. Those things may fall into the category of aggressive behavior, but that's not the kind of aggressiveness that wins games.

Being aggressive means going for the ball. Turning on the afterburners running down the field. Scrambling for the ground ball or standing firm on defense. Trying just a little harder and being a little more determined to force the game to the outcome you prefer. Aggressiveness is giving maximum effort with complete determination. Aggressiveness and good sportsmanship are not mutually exclusive. In fact, the best players know how to be both.

There are all kinds of programs that help teach kids to be assertive, such as martial arts or debate team. Look for classes and activities at your local community centers and schools. Even if you don't see significant improvement in the lacrosse game, your kid will benefit from increased self-confidence and skills gained.

A Broader Definition of Winning

In any lacrosse game, there is only one winner in the classic sense of the word. But it serves kids well to teach them to look beyond that narrow definition of winning and success. A kid who starts a new sport and learns to play it competently is a success. The start-up team that showed dramatic improvement this year from last year is successful. A player who improves his shots on goal is a winner.

In fact, encourage your kid to focus on individual success - things like winning face-offs, increasing the number of assists or saves, or scoring a goal. After all, a player has more control over those. And, it is good for kids to compete against their own potential, to strive to improve at something.

Coping with Failure

Winners are also those who handle failure well and learn from loss. Great players in most sports had their share of failures, losses and set-backs. They just coped well. Diane Geppi-Aikens was told in 1995 that she had a brain tumor and that chemotherapy and radiation wouldn't work. Doctors didn't know how long the Loyola University women's lacrosse coach would live. As the cancer progressed, the formerly athletic Geppi-Aikens eventually ended up coaching from a motorized wheelchair, helping her team deal with the extra pressure from media attention.

In a May, 2003 article on ESPN.com, "It's Not Easy When Mom Has Cancer," by Cynthia Faulkner, Geppi-Aikens said that bringing high school girls into Loyola and sending them out as women, teaching life skills as well as lacrosse skills, was one of her missions in life. Her 2003 team's leading scorer, Suzanne Eyler, said in the article, "She's taught us winning or losing a lacrosse game isn't what's important. Being with the people you love; that's what it's about."

Loyola fell to Princeton in the semifinals of the 2003 Championship Tournament, and Geppi-Aikens passed away a month later. But she continues to influence and inspire a generation of lacrosse players.

Fear of Winning

Sometimes, kids become conflicted about winning. For one thing, when you're on top, everyone is gunning for you. That can be a little scary for a young player. It might seem easier and safer to hang in the middle of the pack, rather than be out in front where you might invite attack.

In our high-pressure society, athletes may pick up the message that if they reach the top, they will have to stay there or others will be disappointed in them. Young players may see professional athletes strutting and gloating, and hear about contract disputes and fights with management, and wonder if they will still be able to be friends with their teammates if the team makes it to the top. Kids might wonder if they can handle the next level of competition, if they can be good enough.

The best way to deflect these fears is to de-emphasize winning and losing from the beginning, to encourage and celebrate effort. Parents can be talking about these kinds of issues all along, always putting the focus on good sportsmanship, teamwork and improvement. Let your child know that your only expectations are that she put in appropriate effort, be a good sport, and have fun.

Process versus Outcome Goals

One player decides his goal is to keep improving his game. Another player wants to win the championship. The first goal is process oriented, the second is outcome oriented. The player has more control and a greater likelihood of success with the process-oriented goal. As the player works to achieve it, he may well also achieve the second player's goal and win that championship, but maybe not.

Encourage your kid to set process-oriented goals, and he will be successful even if the entire goal is not met. A long-term outcome goal, like, say, winning the NCAA championship senior year in college, just has too many external factors that influence the result. If a player doesn't achieve the goal, even if those external factors are largely to blame, he still may feel like a failure. This approach isn't a total loss, however; because such a goal involves the entire team, it can sometimes force players to work hard and make tangible progress in other areas. In other words, the two types of goals can sometimes work together.

With a process goal, though, there is a high degree of correlation between a player's effort and the successful achievement of the goal. Be sure that the goal is measurable, and that the long-term desire can be broken into shorter term pieces.

Playing Friends

In local leagues, camps, and even at school, it is inevitable that kids will eventually have to compete against friends. That can be hard for some kids. Again, if you have been sending the right messages about sports and competition in general, it should be a manageable and even enjoyable situation.

Remind your players that they should give maximum effort in every game, even against a friend, and that doing so helps them both improve, and shows respect. After all, a kid who finds out that a friend took it easy on him on the field would probably feel insulted. Over time, many players will end up on travel teams together, or at the same camp, and the longer kids play lacrosse, the greater the odds that they will know some, if not many, of their opponents.

If everyone plays hard and accepts winning and losing gracefully, it can actually be a lot of fun playing against people you know. Your opponent is no longer a stranger, but a friend you will enjoy talking about the game with afterward. Rivalries become more intense but at the same time more intimate.

Next Coach

Each new season can bring a new coach, as your child moves up in a league or goes from elementary to middle or middle to high school. At younger ages, you are interested in a coach who focuses on getting kids fired up about the game and teaching the basics, but as kids get older, they need a coach who can help them develop.

While the development phase for many sports starts at about adolescence, the timing here depends on when a player started lacrosse. Generally, once a kid knows the game and has mastered it, he is ready to move to the next level. At this point, you want a coach who can bring out a higher level of skill and discipline. You also want a coach with experience teaching kids at this level, as different ages and skill levels have different needs and pose different challenges.

While they probably can't personally choose a coach for the school team, parents can choose when it comes to travel teams, camps and recreational leagues. First be sure that any coach has the basic qualifications for the job, some kind of appropriate training like that from Positive Coaching Alliance (More info: positivecoach.org), and the ability to make practice fun. Then, look for a coach who has worked at this higher level and who has demonstrated a commitment to the team.

The best coaches focus on making individual players and the team better, not on beating a particular opponent. In fact, some strategies for improving players and the team - such as giving a player experience at a new position, giving everyone playing time, or a commitment to developing newer players - may result in coaching decisions that make it more difficult to win that big game.

One parent recalls the effect when a team her child was on abandoned the development philosophy - where the coach gave players time playing different positions and encouraged setting up good plays over scoring goals - in favor of winning more games. The player no longer enjoyed practices or games and, in fact, ended up switching to another sport. The parent, who fully supported her daughter's move, said "I seriously doubt that she'll ever look back on her life and say, gee I wish I'd won more games when I was 12."

Bottom line, a coach should care more about all-around development - psychological, physical, tactical and technical - rather than the win-loss record. In the long run, total player and team development will pay off.

Transitions

Any time a player changes coaches for whatever reason, try to make the transition a positive one. If there are problems or issues, players should be able to approach the coach; in fact, parents should encourage that dialogue. Just be sure your players choose an appropriate time, such as before or after practice and not during it, for example. This goes for parents, too. Generally, asking questions or raising problems is best done in person, too, rather than by phone or email.

It is important for kids to learn to adapt. They may not get along well with every coach, just as they may not like every teacher they have now, or every boss they might have in the future. But learning to adapt to situations that aren't perfect is a good and necessary life skill.

Being Creative

In the late 1980s, a Syracuse lacrosse player named Paul Gait jumped from behind the crease and scored a goal. This move, which became known as the Air Gait, changed the game and showed how players' feet can leave the ground while scoring goals. Although the Air Gait itself was declared illegal, Paul and his brother launched changes to the game.

Some of the greatest improvements in other sports came about because a coach or player chose to break the mold and experiment with unorthodox methods. In lacrosse, that experimentation gave us the cool behind-the-back shot. Of course, developments in technology help advance play, too.

But creativity makes a sport more exciting, and in lacrosse it should be encouraged. Lacrosse is not like football, where every play is tightly scripted. There are certain principles, and a coach will provide a basic framework for plays, such as a 1-3-2 offense or a 1-4-1 offense, but beyond that, good coaches will let their players be creative and improvise.

The fundamentals won't change - speed, accuracy and teamwork - but there is always room for innovation in technique and tactics. Encourage your player to experiment within the framework of the game.

Analyzing Play

One technique that can help lacrosse players develop higher-level game skills is analyzing game films, both their own and those of other teams. This is something a coach, not a parent, should do, but it doesn't hurt for parents to listen in. A coach will be looking for, and pointing out for the players, things like communication among the players on the field, placement on the field, when to take a shot, face-offs, and defensive strategy.

NCAA championship games are great examples of lacrosse athletes competing at the highest level, and all young, aspiring players can learn a great deal watching these games. A player can do this on his own as well. Just remember that Major League Lacrosse is a different game with some different rules, so young players probably should not just be analyzing films of MLL games.

Higher levels of competition help players improve their game, and as players get better, playing becomes more fun. As parents, we can help everyone keep a healthy perspective on competition, encourage good sportsmanship, and support our kids. When we do that, turning up the heat can be a good thing.

6

Encouraging Your Kids
And Keeping Your Friends

"Spinach is good for you. Sports are supposed to be fun."
Coach's son in an episode of Picket Fences

As parents, we want the best for our children, and our goals usually center around helping them be confident, happy, and of good character. Most of us, deep down, want our kids to have a better life than we did. We sometimes forget, though, that children are unique individuals with their own personalities, gifts, desires and dreams - not smaller versions of ourselves and not our second chance to succeed where we may have failed before.

In our high-pressure, status-conscious society, it's no wonder loving parents sometimes turn into pushy ones. Particularly when it comes to sports. But it doesn't have to be that way. Instead of pushing our children, we can encourage them and support them in finding their own way and in fulfilling their own ideas of success.

Parental Goals

Many conflicts between parents and children about sports result from the former confusing their own, usually outcome-oriented, goals with those of the latter. It is easy for parents to do this without even realizing it.

How many times have you heard an otherwise wonderful, loving mom or dad say something like, "I just want to do all that I can to help my child get a lacrosse scholarship." Or, "We just want our child to be the best player." Achieving goals like these are dependent on four things:

✓ the child has to take up lacrosse, and become very dedicated to the sport

✓ the child has to put in the necessary hours of practice and conditioning
✓ the parent has to provide the necessary financial support, and
✓ the parent has to provide the time and emotional support needed.

Clearly, half the action needed to accomplish the goal is dependent upon the child and not the parent. If that child wholeheartedly supports his end of the deal then everything may be fine. But what if a kid decides in high school that she wants to pursue other interests, or divide up time between several activities? Or what if a child, trying to please her parents, dedicates a great deal of her young life to the sport, only to find that her true gifts lie elsewhere?

Pushing a child to excel in hopes of a college scholarship is also likely to lead to disappointment. Consider that in the year 2000, an estimated 35 million children participated in organized youth sports, some 6.5 million played high school interscholastic athletics, and roughly 300,000 participated in college sports programs, with only about half of those receiving any form of athletic scholarship.

In lacrosse specifically, only 54 college teams offer scholarships, and most only a few of them. Not only are those pretty slim odds, but playing solely for tangible benefits like all-star status or a scholarship can suck the fun out of a sport for your child. Children end up burned out, parents are stressed, and everyone is unhappy. On the other hand, participation in lacrosse, or another sport, regardless of skill level, will look great on your child's college application. If she loves the sport and is able to commit a number of years to it, admissions offices will consider this a positive.

Parents can set goals that are specific and directly under their control. For example, "I will provide the financial help for my child to pursue lacrosse as far as he wants." Or, "We will give our child encouragement and support to improve at the sport." These process-oriented goals clarify that the young player is the one in the driver's seat, and the parent plays a supportive role as far as lacrosse involvement is concerned.

Process-oriented goals that parents can set for themselves include:

✓ to highlight the value of lacrosse as a lifetime sport for fun, fitness and skill development
✓ to provide necessary time and financial and emotional support, and
✓ to use lacrosse as a vehicle to teach good attitude, teamwork, discipline and character.

Goals like these will give you a sense of accomplishment, whether your child ultimately decides to take up lacrosse, soccer, theater, music, or whatever. You can use team sports as a catalyst to teach your child life lessons valuable in any arena.

Why We Should Never be 'Pushy'

After years of financially supporting a child's lacrosse habit, driving to lessons and sitting through games, even the most patient parent may start to expect winning results. Parents may feel that because they contribute time and money, they are justified in demanding a winning result. Of course, your child should be contributing time, effort, and perhaps even money as well, and in the end, the results are up to him and the rest of the team - not you, the parent.

It is perfectly reasonable to expect results. Parents should expect positive results from participation in sports, such as a child who is fit, has a better social life, and is learning dedication to an activity. For one thing, this helps you decide whether your time and money is well spent. The key, though, is to measure results not by wins and losses, but by your child's development of good skills and attributes. Keeping your eye on these prizes will make you less likely to get pushy.

Winning is great, but it's not the only desirable outcome. Remember that the ultimate purpose of sports is to provide your child with opportunities for fun and growth. The triumphs and heartaches inherent in sports provide your child with learning experiences and life lessons that will serve her in adulthood.

Ask yourself, is my child learning? Is the game emotionally healthy for her? Has it made him more mature and better prepared for life? If the answers are yes, then your time and money have been well spent, no matter what the team's win/loss record.

After a few years of playing, you can also expect your child's skills to improve. This is a focus on performance, whereas emphasizing wins and losses is focusing on competence. A focus on competence often results in children appearing to fall short of parental expectations. A player may be improving in personal skill, but the team's record is heavy on losses, perhaps because it is playing tough competitors (which is no doubt contributing to that personal improvement). This can cause parents to push their child without even realizing it. Resist that urge. Instead, look at your child's development of new friendships and his or her overall enjoyment of the sport. If the yardsticks you use to measure results are life lessons and improvement in personal skill, chances are you will see great progress.

Parents can also get pushy if they decided early on that they are going to raise a professional lacrosse player, or one who obtains admission to the best college team on scholarship. Making crucial life choices for your child in this way is almost certainly a set-up for disappointment.

Even if your child initially goes along, chances are good that this compliance will not survive the adolescent years or, even worse, your child may rebel against this pre-determined goal in young adulthood. In addition, the pressure this can bring to bear on participation in the sport can take away the fun and turn it into work. When that happens, parents will find they have to push even harder.

Most parents would be ecstatic to see their children reach the pinnacle of a sport. By all means let yourself dream big. Just remember that this is your dream, not your child's. The choice to continue playing in high school or college should be made much later in a child's development. It should be made largely by the player, with the support of parents and any input invited by the child. Parents who can keep the dream of playing in college or professionally in perspective will be less likely to get pushy.

Look at this along with the many other aspirations, equally important, that you have for your child - dreams like a successful and rewarding career, a happy marriage and children, lifelong involvement in a community organization, and other worthwhile pursuits. Finally, separate dreams from goals, and remember that you have control over your own goals and not those of your child.

Playing Up

Opting to "play up," or compete in an older age division, can be a real ego-trip for some parents. But the decision needs to be based on sound reasons.

A mature and competitive kid who is consistently winning probably needs more of a challenge to remain interested, and should compete in a higher division. With younger children, it isn't so clear-cut. A nine-year-old may be consistently displaying better skills than his peers, but you have to consider that he is also having a lot of fun practicing with them. This is especially true if he regularly hangs out with the kids he is playing with. Moving him to an older age group may be great for his game, but will not appeal to him socially. Remember that there is no hurry. If you don't move him up now, he'll have plenty of time to advance later on.

Moving a young child up can also provide him with a convenient excuse for losing. Parents may have a tendency to believe that their child is losing because he is playing in a more competitive level. This rationalization can prevent kids from developing mental toughness.

One of the best ways to take advantage of the benefits of playing up is to "mix it up." For younger children who are consistently outperforming their age group, schedule occasional practices with an older group but continue practices with peers. In these cases, good coaches will avoid creating the impression that one kid is being handpicked for promotion.

Also, kids who play up and either don't enjoy the challenge or aren't ready for it may feel like they are being demoted when the playing up stops. One way to avoid this is for coaches to have playing up as part of the regular program and to do it without a lot of fanfare. Parents can also consider trying this at a summer camp or in private instruction.

Preventing 'I Quit'

Even if you don't play your kid up too soon, aren't a pushy parent, and pretty much do everything right, your kid may eventually want to quit lacrosse, for a variety of reasons. Parents and coaches can keep the desire to quit from surfacing prematurely, or for the wrong reasons, with a number of strategies:

✓ Avoid pushing young kids into a high degree of specialization in a single sport.

✓ Leave the coaching to a professional, as parent coaching can strain your relationship with your child.

✓ Emphasize mastery of the sport over competence. Teach kids to enjoy the process of developing proficiency, and help them measure accomplishments by improvement in various skills rather than that win/loss record.

✓ Help kids learn to deal with loss in a positive way. Emphasize effort over accomplishment.

✓ Find coaches and teams that emphasize fun and good sportsmanship.

✓ Encourage your child to practice enough to develop good skills -anything is more fun when you're good at it - but don't overdo it. Be sure your child has balanced interests and time for other important things like family.

✓ Be prepared to lessen the degree of parental involvement in decision-making as your child gets older.

✓ Use private lessons to help a child with self-esteem and skills, if difficulty mastering them is part of the problem.

Final Choice

Even if you've done all the right things, at some point your child may want to quit anyway. For an adolescent, leaving lacrosse, or another sport or skill, may be one way of asserting independence. A teen who perceives that his parents want him to play may rebel against that. Or it may be that a teen just decides he no longer really likes or enjoys the game, or that there is something else that is more important. The bottom line is that parents should be prepared for the possibility that one day their child may want to quit.

Always remember that the choice to play must always be your child's. All you can do is gently nudge children in the direction you want them to go. When young children express interest in lacrosse, sign them up for a season or camp and let them give the sport a chance. Make them stick with it through the season or session. This teaches children that it is important to finish a project or commitment that they have started. Often, after a few practices, kids become more proficient and aren't always chasing the ball around, and they want to continue.

Younger children may be confused about the rules, and parents can explain the rules or practice with their kids to help them feel more comfortable. Kids can learn a valuable lesson by following through on what they start even when they don't particularly enjoy it. Be sympathetic but firm about finishing whatever the child committed to. Once the session is over, then you can allow your child to move on.

Older children may have more complex reasons for wanting to quit, but may need your help articulating those reasons. Talk to the coach. One of the following reasons may apply:

1. Lacrosse isn't fun anymore. If this applies, make sure the coach is compatible with your child, and don't be afraid to try a new one. Maybe the competition has become too intense too soon. If so, scale back and focus on more casual participation.
2. There's too much pressure. This could be coming from a parent, coach, or teammates. It may be time for parents to get out of the advice business and leave training to the coach. Maybe the school team needs bonding and fun activities outside of practice. Encourage your child to spend more time on other hobbies.
3. There isn't enough time. Many child development experts recommend focusing on one or at most two

extra-curricular activities at a time, but in our over-scheduled society most children are involved in multiple ones. Help your child prioritize. Select one sport and hold off on others until the season is over or a camp opportunity comes up.

4. I'm not good enough. If your child gives this reason, he may have been played up too soon, or placed on a team where the skill levels don't match up. You may need to go back a bit so she'll learn the basics a bit better, either on another team, at a camp or with a private instructor.

Once you've exhausted all these strategies and your child still wants to quit, remember that the time spent involved in lacrosse provided valuable experience, and the decision to move on is itself a life lesson. There is also the chance that a child who is allowed to quit without pushing from the parents will want to return in a few years.

Parental Roles

Parents play an important role - supporting their lacrosse player, with love, money, guidance, motivation, encouragement, time, and transportation. Generally, a parent's involvement should focus on financial and emotional support, character development and education. Parents are important teachers of goal setting and discipline, too.

Parental support can be a determining factor in whether a kid stays healthy, fit and injury-free. Parents can insist on proper warm-up and stretches before and after practice. They can have a huge influence on diet, simply through what food is kept in the house and where the family eats. Get in the habit of driving past the fast food joints; a peanut butter and jelly sandwich and apple beat the burger and fries any day.

Parents can also help keep the weekly workouts fun with routines like medicine balls, hula hoops, skipping rope, shooting baskets on the driveway, family bike rides and other enjoyable activities. It helps when parents lead an active lifestyle, eat well and get plenty of rest, too. Just like your mother told you.

Encourage your children to dream. Inspire them. Tell them stories of all the impossible things that have been accomplished by people following their dreams - people like Homer Hickam, Jr., subject of the movie "October Sky." Homer and a few of his friends, high school students in coal mining country in West Virginia in the 1950s, successfully launched a functional rocket and earned college scholarships, but it took an awful lot of explosions and overcoming the doubts of most of the grown-ups around them.

There are lots of other movies with similar inspiring messages such as "Rudy," "Glory Road" and "Cool Runnings." Watch them with your kids and encourage them to talk about their own dreams. At the same time, when they dream big, encourage them to measure their success by goals accomplished, not by dreams realized. With this practical approach, they will learn to relish true progress in life, even if all those big dreams don't come true.

Work to keep your children interested in lacrosse, and other sports, whether or not you think they have the ability needed for the sport at that particular time. Development occurs in fits and starts, especially before puberty but even beyond. Encourage children to persist even when they feel that they lack natural talent.

Remember that Michael Jordan didn't make that high school basketball team his sophomore year. It would be a shame for a kid to drop out of sports before finding out just how good she can be. Again, the best thing parents can do is focus on lacrosse mastery over winning and losing.

Kids who compete against their own ability are less likely to get caught up in comparison with other kids during the growth phase. Physical changes can lead to uneven performance on some days. Support your kid through these ups and downs. And always encourage kids to have other interests and not make one thing - even if it is lacrosse - their entire life.

Encouragement

Kids love any activity they're good at. Of course, becoming good requires practice. As long as practice is fun, kids will have no problem. Sometimes they need to practice skills that are a little hard to learn, and it isn't so fun. During these times, parents need to provide a lot of encouragement to help kids stick with it.

Help kids find fun things to work on, like behind the back passes or between the leg shots, to keep them motivated. Keep sending positive messages to help your child through the low points. Here are some ways to do that:

1. Set expectations that emphasize healthy values that will help your child become successful and happy. For example, focus on hard work, responsibility, cooperation, patience and persistence, rather than grades or outcomes.
2. Allow your child to experience all emotions. Don't dismiss any feelings, or placate or distract your child from them. Help kids to identify, understand and express their emotions in a healthy way.
3. Actively manage your child's environment and activities - peer interactions, achievement activities, cultural experiences, leisure pursuits - in ways that reflect the values, attitudes and behaviors you want your child to adopt.
4. Create options from which a child can choose.
5. Help children find something they love and are passionate about, and they will be successful and happy.

Achieving success in almost anything requires sustained effort that will always have highs and lows. The trick is to maximize the highs and ride out the lows, and your steady encouragement of your child can make the difference.

7

It's All About The Game

"Keep focused on what you can control - effort, attitude - and don't concern yourself with the things you can't - like weather, field conditions, refs and other players. Anyone can come up with an excuse whey they can't win."
Brian Ferry, Ithaca College All American

On game day, the long hours of practice and conditioning are put to the test. Little things add up when it comes to making sure your child has a fun and successful game. It's always a good idea to check equipment the previous day and get a good rest the night before. Arrive at the field in plenty of time, well-fueled and hydrated, with a positive mental attitude, players and parents as well.

Translating Practice to Game
Game day can present many factors to worry about - a new field, an unknown opponent, a school assignment that is due the next day. Consistent and focused practice is the best preparation for the distractions and nerves that are part of game day.

A player who feels competent will have more confidence. Parents and coaches should stay focused and relaxed, as their attitude will affect how players start the game. Pre-game rituals, and perhaps a bad joke or two, can help lessen the tension.

Preparation
You won't find many collegiate or professional players who party all night long and head straight out to a game early the next morning. If they do, it's practically guaranteed that they won't be doing it for long without their game suffering. Most players follow more helpful pre-game rituals that help them prepare to do their best. One college goalie, for example, always wears his shades

during warm-ups. Another player pulls on wristbands with the team colors. A pre-game ritual can be any kind of activity like this that reminds a player, it's game time. Just be sure to keep it positive.

The day before a game shouldn't be an ordeal, of course. Help your child establish a set of simple, easy to follow routines and, over time, these will become habits that help your child get ready physically and mentally for important games and, later, other important events in life.

As a parent, you play an important role in helping your children develop appropriate on-field behavior and mental toughness. Teach them these important elements to use in games:

- ✓ Focus - concentrate during the game, ignoring fans and taunts.
- ✓ Breathe - during slow times in the game, take a deep breath and think about what you can do better and how you can exploit the opponent's weakness. Sometimes a player can get so wound up, he forgets the simple parts of the game.
- ✓ Loosen up - be aware of tenseness in the body and relax, physically and mentally.
- ✓ Posture - communicate confidence through body language. Shoulders back, head high, purposeful stride.
- ✓ Self-talk - avoid negative self-talk after mistakes, congratulate yourself after a good move.

According to Jill Albee, former Division I women's lacrosse player, "the moment you step on the field you have to tell yourself and believe you are the best player on the field even if you are not. Be confident, not cocky."

At one time or another, most athletes have had the experience of not making a play when it mattered most – known as choking. Choking can usually be attributed to worrying too much about the end result of a game. Learning to forget past mistakes and focus on the here and now is an important skill that kids will need for games and, in fact, for almost any task in life.

The more any of us deal with pressure-filled situations, the better we get at it. Learning, playing and enjoyment are all enhanced by the ability to stay focused on the present. Both parents and coaches can help kids learn to be more aware in this way. Kids won't learn mental fitness skills just by listening to us talk about them though. The skills must be woven into drills and activities.

There are established drills for working on mental toughness and focus. For example, kids can work with a shooting trainer, trying to hit the same spot in the net ten times, working on mental focus and persistence. Talk to the coach about other appropriate drills that can be incorporated into practice or used at home.

At any time you suspect family issues or school problems are affecting your child's ability to concentrate, address those problems as soon as possible. This, of course, is important for your child's overall well-being, not just his lacrosse play.

Twenty-four Hours Before

Maintain a high-carb diet before a grueling game: whole-grain breads, cereals and pasta, plus fruit and vegetables. Avoid fatty and spicy foods. Encourage kids to pack everything into the game bag the night before - all their equipment clean and in working order, spare clothes, and anything else they will need, including the MP3 player. Many athletes have a few favorite songs that get them fired up for a game and in the right mental state of mind, which is plenty of confidence mixed with a little nervousness and excitement.

Be sure kids get plenty of sleep the night before, but not too much, which can actually make them sluggish. In general, you want kids to stick to their regular schedule and amount of sleep. Sometimes, kids suffer from butterflies before a big game and may have trouble getting to sleep. Let them know it is okay to lose some sleep in this way once in a while and that they don't need to freak out.

If there is team practice the day before a game, it should be short and not very intense. Many coaches will even have boys just wear gloves and helmets to keep it low-key. This is a time to allow muscles to recharge and repair in order to maximize performance on game day.

Fueling for the Game

Go bananas. And nuts and chicken salad, peanut butter, or pasta. These are all easy to prepare or are right-out-of-the-box foods parents can offer their kids to make sure they are well fueled on game day. These high-carbohydrate foods help the body store glycogen in the muscles and liver as fuel for activity. Continue to avoid fatty and spicy foods.

Have kids eat three or four hours before a game so the food is completely absorbed from the stomach. A big, all-the-way chili dog right before a game is a bad idea, for obvious reasons. With back-to-back games or at tournaments, good light snacks for between games are things like trail mix, rice cakes, power bars, fruit popsicles, bagels and yogurt.

Hydration is very important for kids, both before, during, and after games. Young children especially need plenty of water; their higher surface-area-to-body-weight ratios cause them to gain more heat from the environment on hot days and lose more heat to a cold day. They also produce more metabolic heat from activity, and have a much lower sweating capacity. All of this can contribute to overheating and even heat stroke.

The American Academy of Pediatrics recommends that a child weighing 88 pounds drink five ounces of cold water every 20 minutes or so, and that one weighing 132 pounds drink nine ounces every 20 minutes. Add an ounce per hour when it is 90 degrees or higher and when kids are active.

Cold water is absorbed by the body faster than warm water. Plain tap water is what your kid needs, but it is fine if you add a little pure fruit juice for flavor. Sports drinks can actually contain a lot of unneeded sugar and other ingredients, so check labels. These can also be expensive; one way to stretch your dollar is to mix half plain water and half sports drink. Avoid drinks with caffeine and phosphoric acid, a chemical found in most colas, which inhibits the body's ability to absorb calcium and also breaks down tooth enamel.

Game Day

When a game is in the afternoon or evening, kids may need some distraction to avoid getting nervous. Suggest a cat nap or a board game. For early games, be sure kids wake up a few hours before so they are fully awake and ready to go at the face-off. All day, your player should be focused on the game and the competition. Coaches often have given your team scouting reports on the opposing team, and players can review them to familiarize themselves with the competition and what they are likely to encounter in the game.

Coaches will usually want kids at the field about an hour before the game. Be sure to find out when your child's coach wants the team to arrive, and be on time. Generally, the team will gather on one side of the field and parents will hang out on the other.

Tell your kid to have a good time, and then spend the waiting time getting to know other parents. Lasting friendships between players, and parents as well, often spring from team sports. At the very least, you can swap information on the latest lacrosse gear sale and arrange carpools to practice. If you have a tendency to get wound up before a game, bring a book to read or crossword puzzle to help you stay relaxed. Kids don't need to see their parents full of the jitters.

The team will do stretches and warm-ups and the coach will probably run through game strategy and give a pep talk, too. The pre-game talk is an important opportunity for the coach to energize the team and promote team work. For a struggling team, the coach can use this time to focus players on achievable goals for this particular game. Meeting those goals can be encouraging to a developing team, no matter what the final score.

Many games for young players will be on school days. Kids obviously need to be in school, and should go to all classes and be sure to complete all assignments even on game days. Most schools have rules about attendance and playing sports, so teach your children the importance of balance early on.

Etiquette

Good etiquette is important in all social situations. In a game setting, it helps everyone have a good time and enjoy some fun, healthy competition.

Parent etiquette requires that you remain relatively calm and stick to positive and encouraging cheering from the sidelines - things like "great shot" and "go Knights!" Applaud points made by both sides - although it's okay if you are a little louder when cheering for your kid's team.

Don't coach from the sidelines, yell instructions or criticism at your kid or other players, and never yell at or berate coaches, players or officials. If you have a real problem with a coaching decision, take it up directly with the coach after the game. Or even better, the next day, in a calm and adult manner.

If you have an issue with the officiating, there are proper steps to take to address them constructively. Talk to your coach or a tournament organizer and they can put you in touch with the official assigner. Chasing after a ref following a game will only make you look like a crazy parent.

Officials are only human and yes, they make mistakes, but it is a pretty safe bet that, over the course of a season or two, the calls that go against you and those that go your way pretty much even out. It's only natural that you tend to remember the ones that go against you more. One of the best ways to appreciate the difficulty of the officiating job is to try it yourself.

No matter what the outcome of the game, congratulate any players you pass on the way to the parking lot, and tell your kid you enjoyed watching the game. Mistakes will happen, guaranteed. Good athletes learn from them. Don't offer your analysis of the game or his play unless asked.

Coach etiquette is sometimes dictated by rules as well as courtesy. Some leagues ban coaching during a game, except at half-time or in time-outs. For the most part, coaching from the sidelines is ineffective, anyway. The best players are those who learn to think on their feet and make their own decisions on the field. It is also nearly impossible for a player to hear an instruction from the sideline, process it mentally and respond in time for it to do any good.

A good coach will make observations about the game and the team to use constructively in a subsequent practice. He will never berate players in front of each other, or yell at the other coach or officials. It is a coach's job to provide instruction and constructive feedback. But good coaches know how to say it and when. And they are always positive and encouraging no matter what the scoreboard says.

Player etiquette requires that players stay loose, have fun, and play their best. Players should never yell at other players, coaches, spectators or officials. Trash talk doesn't belong on a lacrosse field. Should players encounter an opponent who talks trash, their best response is to keep their own mouths closed and play well.

During the Game

As a parent, your job during the game is to cheer for the team and to look for a good play or evidence of extra effort for which you can compliment your child and other players after the game.

Players who are not on the field should still be focused on the game, evaluating the opponent and paying attention to strategies being used. Players should stay in order on the bench so they'll be ready to substitute quickly and effectively. They should also cheer for the players on the field.

A coach's job during the game is to make observations that can be used to instruct the team later. He can note problems or changes in strategy to point out during half time. The coach also pays attention to substitutions and the clock.

After the Game

After a game, players on each team should shake hands and tell each other "good game." Many teams have a short cheer used to thank their opponent. If you pass the officials on your way to your car, thank them for their time and hard work. Save the game analysis for later; say something positive to your kid, take her out for a treat, and just relax and talk about other things. Later, be sure your player reflects on what lessons she can learn from the game. Always emphasize effort over the score and fun above all.

Kids will probably need some carbohydrates within 30 minutes of a game to refuel their bodies. Take care of any soreness or minor injuries with stretching and ice, and handle any problems with equipment while it is fresh on your mind. A good night's sleep after a game is important, too.

Games are the big payoff for your kid's hard work. They can also be a lot of fun for Mom and Dad. Wear your team's color and make lots of positive noise. And don't forget, sunscreen and water are important for spectators, too.

8

College Lacrosse: The Big Time

*"College lacrosse is the best time of your life. The people you
meet you know will be your friends for life.
It's a great environment."*
Justin Smith, professional player, Philadelphia Barrage;
3-time NCAA College Champion;
Division III Player of the Year

Most parents whose kids play sports well find themselves,
at some point, thinking "college scholarship." There's
nothing wrong with that, as long as those parents don't
start saying "college scholarship" out loud to a sixth
grader. There are many good, positive reasons for kids to
play sports, and playing in college is a great long-term
goal for kids.

College play is high-level competition, and that is a
lot of fun for an athlete. Life-long friendships are made
with teammates. There is interesting and exciting travel to
other colleges, tournaments and special events.

Many high school lacrosse players probably have
dreams of being on a college team, and even of being
recruited and getting a scholarship. But that's the point: it
needs to be your kid's dream, and not yours. Kids who
feel pressured to do well in order to get a scholarship are
likely to feel stress and even burn out, and parents will
end up disappointed. The hard feelings this scenario
creates may never be completely overcome.

For a kid who loves lacrosse, college play is a
worthwhile and achievable dream. Knowing a little about
the recruiting process and college-level play will help a
player decide if this is his or her dream, and offer players
and families some guidance for working to make that
dream come true.

US College Recruiting

So far, lacrosse in the US has avoided the frenzied scramble for spots on college teams that have turned some other sports into intense pressure cookers for players, families and coaches as early as ninth grade. Most of the players on college lacrosse teams right now didn't commit to a college until early fall or even spring of their senior year.

There are signs, though, that this is changing, that as lacrosse becomes more popular, it is moving in the direction of those other sports. Andrew Combs, assistant coach at Towson College, reports that more and more high school athletes are looking at college earlier and earlier. For the 2005 lacrosse season, college coaches were finished with recruiting by September, and teams for the 2006 season were wrapped up by August. Combs attributes the earlier decisions in part to the huge growth of the sport in high school, and the small number of spots available on teams. Earlier decisions can be fine, as long as kids are making them for good reasons, not because of pressure from coaches or peers. There are things parents and players can do to avoid potential pitfalls.

Encourage your kid to choose a college based on the overall picture. Take lacrosse out as a factor for just a moment and make sure the fit is right. Kids are students first, then athletes. Decide what matters most in a college, and find that first. You never know, your kid could injure a knee the first game and never play again, simply decide college sports are too serious, or get involved in something else entirely.

It could also be a mistake for a young player to choose a college for a particular coach. Coaches move around, and that admired figure could be gone by the time your kid gets to campus. In short, get all the information your kid needs to make a decision, no matter what pressure is being put on him. Be sure your kid picks a school that will be right for him after college. Finally, be honest with any coaches and colleges your player is considering.

Some perspective on the whole college recruiting picture is important. It is a coach's job to win. Those who don't may not be in coaching for long. To win, a coach needs to secure talent. Recruiting that talent can become a race among coaches to lock up particular players before someone else does. It is this race that can lead to situations where kids as young as 16 and 17 - and their families - are being asked to make very important decisions under a lot of pressure.

Early decisions make life easier for coaches, and deciding early can get a kid into a better school or onto a better team before all the spots are taken, but it isn't always necessarily a good thing for kids. It will be up to parents to keep the best interests of their kids at the forefront.

Sometimes the pressure comes from peers. When his best friend has committed to Maryland, it's hard for a high school player not to feel pressure to get his own spot lined up. Kids can feel this pressure even earlier, which can have negative effects, such as leading a kid to quit all other sports in order to play more lacrosse. Nearly all college coaches still oppose specialization and encourage students to play at least one other sport. College lacrosse recruiting still favors the multi-sport athlete, and parents should remember that playing several sports has many other benefits for their kids.

Early, verbal commitments are not binding, and neither are scholarship offers made prior to the signing of National Letters of Intent (NLI), which usually occurs during a specific week in late November of the prospect's senior year. These letters bind student athletes to a college for one academic year and bind the college as well, to whatever scholarship offer it has presented. The NLI program was founded by the Collegiate Commissioners Association to protect both parties from the problems of last-minute changes of heart on either side. More than 500 universities participate (More info: national-letter.org).

College Visits

The National Collegiate Athletic Association (NCAA. More info: ncaa.org) allows colleges to host prospects on official visits to campus beginning the first day of senior year. Often, these visits are paid for by the college and involve tours of campus, attending class, meeting with coaches, and staying with a current team member for two nights.

These are potentially very valuable to a kid trying to decide if she fits in at a particular college and with a particular team. After all, kids will be spending a lot of time with college teammates, and a good fit is important. The official visit and the opportunities it offers are lost when kids make early decisions. This may be fine if a kid is already familiar with a college and the team, but don't equate a one-night visit to a campus that may include watching a game and shaking the hand of a few players with a true official visit. Encourage your kid to get to know the team and coaches before committing years of his or her life to them.

Official visits are typically only offered by Division I teams. Of course, if an invitation for an official visit isn't forthcoming, go ahead and make a visit on your own. It will still be very valuable for your player to see the campus and meet the coach and team. And while Division III programs can't offer the same benefits, they are also excellent programs that compete nationally.

Players need to have realistic expectations about campus visits, and parents shouldn't be shy about ensuring that any visits will be appropriately supervised. Think about it; your 17- or 18-year-old high school student will be spending the night on a college campus. Talk to her about the importance of getting an accurate read on a school, which would include a sense of the academic environment and regular campus life in addition to the social aspects. Some kids may be tempted to experience the wild side of college a bit early, and while coaches and admissions officials take their responsibility for these young visitors seriously, the reality is that they aren't with recruits every minute of a visit.

Remind your kid that the goal of a visit is to determine his interest in a particular school, and that institution's interest in him. Getting carried away with the whole college weekend experience won't be conducive to either of those.

Resist the urge to accept invitations for overnight visits for your junior in high school. Opt for a day-long visit instead, ending no later than 10 p.m. As one college coach put it, anything a 16-year-old could learn on a college campus after 11 p.m. isn't something he needs to know. Not yet, anyway.

Club Lacrosse

High school teams are not the only places for players to be seen by college coaches; in fact, they may not always be the best places. Lacrosse camps, club teams and off-season tournaments offer important exposure. For players from other countries who want to play on a US college team, these will be critical.

While US colleges do some recruiting in Canada and at the World Games for players from other countries, for the most part, players will need to make themselves visible. College coaches are at camps and clubs, looking at and evaluating players. Players also benefit from instruction, recruiting tips and the level of competition at these events.

For several years, Ricky Sowell, head coach at St. John's University, has checked out potential players at the Adrenaline Lacrosse Sonoma Shootout, held each summer in California. These camps offer important opportunities for players to showcase themselves, he says, especially for those who aren't from the East Coast. College coaches simply need to see someone play, he adds.

Stats, letters, even game films, just aren't the same as seeing someone actually play. For one thing, a coach can see what kind of competition the player is facing. For another, he can observe a player's attitude. Coaches look for talent and speed, of course, but perhaps more important is the attitude - competitive desire, a passion to succeed. If a player has that passion, a coach can develop the lacrosse skills. Sowell also loves to see kids who have played two or three different sports.

One potential downside to club teams and summer tournaments is that they create an opportunity for players to feel that college decision pressure. If one player at a big camp or tournament has committed, it can make other players feel anxiety and a sense of urgency. Parents can help balance this trend.

For top players, getting onto a US college team will be no problem. Division II and III players, especially those who are not from the East Coast, will have to seek out a college team, and grades will continue to be important.

Put Me In, Coach

Summer camps increasingly offer an opportunity for lacrosse players to showcase their talents in front of college coaches. And kids from all over are doing so successfully. Conrad Clevlen, a middie who graduated from McNeil High School in Austin, Texas, signed to play NCAA Division II lacrosse at Notre Dame de Namur University in Southern California.

NDNU coach Joseph Romano saw Clevlen play at the Sonoma Shootout in Northern California and stayed in touch. A big selling point for Romano: the high school coach spoke well of Clevlen as a person and an athlete.

College Scholarships

The best advice for kids hoping to snag a scholarship is, get your grades up as high as possible and keep them there! Good grades, an exemplary player record, and good sportsmanship may well land your player a college scholarship, especially if he keeps the options open - another state, Division II or III, partial scholarships and so forth.

The number of NCAA scholarships for lacrosse at the Division I level is small, but there are many other types of scholarships available. High school counselors can provide information on scholarships.

Even if kids have other plans and aren't remotely interested in college, encourage them to go through the college admission and scholarship processes. Then when that big fat envelope comes in the mail, with an actual offer, your kid may decide college sounds pretty good after all.

True cost of college

According to the College Board, the average annual cost of tuition and fees alone at four-year public colleges for 2004 -2005 was nearly $6000. Add room and board, and the total cost jumps to more than $12,000. Private schools, of course, can cost much more.

Fortunately, there are sources of help; in fact, the average grant aid per college student is growing, the College Board reports. Almost $134 billion in student aid was distributed for the academic year 2005-06, with students also borrowing more than $17 billion from nonfederal sources (More info: collegeboard.com). Families also get a break on federal income tax for saving for college and on tuition payments.

Lacrosse Numbers

More than 108,000 high school students were playing lacrosse at about 2,600 schools according to a recent survey by the National Federation of State High School Associations (More info: nfhs.org). Many of these are seniors who may be planning to continue enjoying lacrosse in college.

Some 221 colleges have men's lacrosse and 175 have women's lacrosse teams, in NCAA Divisions I, II and III. The different divisions have to do with the number of men's and women's sports offered at an institution, with contest and participant minimums. Division I institutions, for example, must sponsor at least seven sports for men and seven for women, with two team sports for each gender, must play all of the minimum number of games against Division I opponents, and meet some minimum attendance requirements. Division III schools must sponsor at least five sports each for men and women, with two team sports. This level features an emphasis on the participants rather than the spectators, and most student athletes receive no financial aid related to their athletic ability.

In addition, there are 180 men's and 172 women's club teams at colleges, as well as community college and junior college teams. This number of college teams translates to at least 26,000 college lacrosse players. Assuming that about a quarter of them graduate each year, some 6,000 high school graduates are needed each year to fill those slots on college lacrosse teams. A team will take anywhere from five to 20 players a year, depending on openings and recruiting strategies.

As lacrosse grows at the youth level, competition for this more or less fixed number of openings will become more intense, especially at the top levels. Some teams take more players than they need, since coaches can't always be sure who will actually show up and who won't, so check into this before committing. Many college players benefit from some sort of financial aid. Each NCAA Division I school, however, has a maximum of only 12 scholarships for men and 12 for women in lacrosse.

The Road to College

Planning ahead will give your child the greatest number of options and will help your family make sound decisions about college and other future choices. A child's freshman year of high school is when parents, kids and coaches should start gathering information and working on a plan. Your child will likely make a final decision in the first half of his or her senior year. In between, there are a lot of things you can do to make that decision one that will give your child a good start on life.

Getting into college isn't easy these days, and some are harder to get into than others. Stay on top of things and it will all go more smoothly.

Freshman Year

Have your child collect information about the college admission and financial aid processes. The high school counselor can be a big help with this. The NCAA has a Guide for the College-Bound Student Athlete that can be downloaded from the website (More info: ncaa.org) or ordered by phone (800-638-3731).

The NCAA also requires certain core courses, so make a list of those and be sure your player takes them in high school. With the school counselor's help, compile a list of at least 10 to twenty colleges that interest your child.

Collect basic information from these colleges; websites are a good place to start. If you have any special circumstances, such as home schooling, contact the colleges to inquire about policies on these. If your child is on a junior varsity team this year, that's great. Junior Varsity players are likely to get more playing time than they would on varsity, which helps them develop faster and build confidence.

Sophomore Year

Be sure your student takes the PSAT/NMSQT test (More info: collegeboard.com). This test is valuable preparation for the SAT, and the results automatically put your child in the running for National Merit Scholarships. When the family travels, take advantage of opportunities to visit any of the colleges on your list.

Beginning this year, or even freshman year, consider the exposure offered to college coaches when you select summer and off-season lacrosse camps - and be sure to sign up for some kind of summer play. Start compiling information that will be helpful when applying to college, such as your player's record, newspaper clippings, letters of recommendation, references from any internships, jobs or sponsorships. It can be a good thing to be on a junior varsity team this year, too.

Junior Year

Take the SAT and, possibly, the ACT. Report these scores to the NCAA Clearinghouse, and register with the Clearinghouse at the end of the year. Continue visiting colleges and refining your list. Contact the admissions offices when visiting and get an official tour; this will be an opportunity to meet admissions people and others who can help you later on.

Meet with coaches, too, and for the schools at the top of your kid's list, keep in touch after the visit to communicate interest. Select a summer camp that will maximize your kid's exposure to the right coaches. This will most likely be your player's last chance to be seen by a coach, unless you decide on a post-graduate year, since by the time lacrosse season rolls around senior year, college commitments will already be made.

Senior Year

Early in the year, apply to the top five or ten colleges on your list. While most colleges have application fees, some waive these if you apply by a certain date, or for online applications. Meet with the high school counselor to discuss how your child can best present himself or herself on applications. Be sure your child requests letters of recommendation from teachers and coaches - and works on those essays. Investigate and apply for scholarships. High school counselors have a lot of information on these, too.

In the fall of the year, students begin receiving National Letters of Intent or offers from schools. Don't let the best financial aid package weigh too heavily in your decision. Experts advise selecting a college based on the academic strength of the school first of all, then the size and location, the quality of the coach and team, the graduation rate for student athletes, and the scholarship money as just one of the criteria.

Scholarships are awarded on a year-by-year basis, and if a student gets little or no money freshman year, that doesn't mean she won't be offered more the next year.

After Graduation

Be sure your high school counselor mails final transcripts to the NCAA Clearinghouse and colleges.

Post-graduate Year

This basically amounts to repeating senior year, on purpose. It is a good opportunity for those who want to develop more in the classroom and on the field. Take this time to work on fitness, improve grades, and search for a college that fits your child best, both academically and for lacrosse.

Homeschooling

In some sports, homeschooling is a way to create a flexible schedule for a child to make it easier to pursue the sport more seriously. In lacrosse, association with a high school team will generally be very valuable for a player, creating opportunity to participate in an appropriate level of competition, be part of a team, and gain easy exposure to college coaches. In many places, high school teams are club or intramural sports, though, and a player doesn't necessarily have to attend the school to be on the team.

Lacrosse Taking More States by Storm

California, Texas and Colorado have seen a lot of lacrosse action in recent years. Now Florida is catching up - and your state may be next.

Florida is the fourth most populous state in the country, and the scene of a lacrosse boom. The number of youth players in the state increased from 980 to 2,805 in just four years, according to US Lacrosse. The sport is very close to qualifying to be sanctioned by the state, which will fuel its growth even more. Sanctioned status will allow lacrosse to organize a state title and will lift limits on the number of students playing.

St. Leo University recently fielded Florida's first NCAA varsity team, in Division II, and other schools are considering adding the sport. Florida high schools have already contributed players to Division I teams, including the University of Massachusetts, Yale University and Bucknell University.

Homeschooling is not a euphemism for dropping out, and it shouldn't mean reducing school hours or substituting more lacrosse. Good homeschooling means a parent has chosen to be teacher, administrator and parent all rolled into one. The parent has to maintain the same number of hours for academic teaching as a public or private school.

For a kid, homeschooling means increased self-discipline and adjusting to a different schedule for socialization. When you and your child understand these basic tenets, and if you both can make the necessary adjustments, then and only then should you consider homeschooling. Contact your local school district and area homeschooling organizations and find out as much as you can about the requirements and realities before taking the leap.

Parents of homeschooled kids who want to play lacrosse in college need to be diligent about documenting lacrosse experience, getting references from coaches and so forth. Homeschooled students should register with the NCAA Initial-Eligibility Clearinghouse after graduation (More info: ncaa.clearinghouse.net). You'll need to send in standardized test scores, transcript, proof of high school graduation, evidence that homeschooling was conducted in accordance with the law, and a list of textbooks used. Parents should be sure that their students take the required number of core courses in the right subjects to qualify for NCAA eligibility.

There are several thousand colleges out there, and some of the ones you've never heard of do the best job of preparing young men and women to be successful in life. Not everyone can get into the big universities, nor are these the right place for everyone. Spend some time making that list of potential colleges, and be open to putting some small but wonderful institutions on it. Of course, if those places offer lacrosse, at any level, so much the better.

9

Financing A Lacrosse Habit

"Fundraising places a burden on the team as a whole, but it can unite and strengthen a team, too. It is encouraging to know that we are responsible for our funds and that we have a duty to ourselves and those who supported us to give the season our best efforts."
Ernst Leiss, starting defenseman, University of Texas, two-time All-American.

Playing sports is lots of fun for kids, and for parents. We know it's good for them, too. But having a kid who is serious about sports usually hits the old pocketbook pretty hard. For lacrosse, equipment is one of the main expenses. Of course, once you have the basic stuff, it costs nothing to play wall ball all day, or collect a few friends for a pick-up game on the local field. Still, to provide the support needed to help your child develop his or her game, a little budgeting and planning ahead is wise.

At the higher levels of play, there are the costs of summer camps, college camps, and club teams. Club dues range from $450 to $700 per year, and camps can cost anywhere from $150 to $750 per session. Camp can also involve travel and accommodation expenses in addition to registration. If local camps are available, they may be more affordable, but depending on your player's level and goals, a distant camp may be a better investment. Your younger player will probably go to camp to improve lacrosse skills, make some friends, and have fun. Players at higher levels may also want to consider camps that offer exposure to college coaches.

Holding Down Expenses
Major manufacturers of lacrosse equipment, such as Warrior, Brine, and STX, support player development by

offering discounts on equipment and free clothing to top-ranked club teams competing at the higher levels. For the rest of us, it's cash, check or credit card.

The Good News

The wholesale sale of sporting goods equipment, sports apparel and athletic footwear totaled $55 billion in 2005, according to the Sporting Goods Manufacturers Association. Many parents feel they have contributed more than their fair share to that total, what with the latest equipment and performance apparel every kid seems to want. It is important to be creative with purchases in order to keep costs down. Your efforts can also teach your child important life lessons about money, budgeting, and choices.

It is possible to make economical choices with some lacrosse equipment, depending on the level of play and the age of your player. In fact, with younger players, you'll want to avoid top-of-the-line in some areas, since they are likely to outgrow certain pieces fairly quickly.

Don't Skimp on the Stick

You'll want to make sure the equipment you buy is adequate to do the job it is intended to do, of course. The lacrosse stick is one place you won't want to skimp. That doesn't mean you have to buy the highest priced stick, either. Look for quality models in the mid-price range, which are perfect for your child's growing years when she may go through a stick every year or two. Your local lacrosse store may have good buys on a mid-priced stick; look for deals on the internet and at used sports equipment stores, too.

Take advantage of your child's network of friends, too. They may know kids who have decided to move on to another sport, or to a different stick. Coaches may be a good source for this stick networking. By the same token, let them know if you have equipment that is available, too.

Sticks simply wear out, get broken or lost. That's why players should keep a re-stringing kit on hand, and a back-up stick prepped and ready to go.

Bank on the Team

Some companies and retail stores may offer discounts on equipment, shoes, and attire for recreational teams, especially for a team purchase. If your kid's team doesn't already do this, ask the coach about purchasing things like helmets as a team in order to get a discount. As a rule, club teams make group purchases on equipment and offer players discounts.

Saving on Lessons

Sign up for semi-private sessions instead of private ones. Pairing your player up with another one will not only save you money, your kid is likely to have more fun with someone else his age to learn and practice with. Besides, a full lesson one-on-one may be too much for a young child to handle. Rather than sign up for half-hour lessons, switch to a one-hour, semi-private lesson with another player, or a group lesson with several players.

Hour for hour, camps are generally less expensive and offer the opportunity for players to put everything together that might be learned in a private lesson. You should, however, shop around for camps. Local day camps will, of course, be less expensive than overnight camps that require travel. At some point, your player may reach a higher level of play where the prestige of the camp, the level of coaching and even the presence of college coaches will make that distant camp a worthwhile investment. But for younger players, the local camps are more than adequate for learning and improving skills, making friends and having fun. Getting to know players from other parts of town will make future games even more fun and competitive.

Earning It

Consider ways that your player can earn money to help with lacrosse expenses. Young kids still love the old-fashioned lemonade stand. Kids can offer to pet sit for neighbors, rake leaves, wash cars or perform other chores. Older kids can mow lawns or baby sit. High school students can get part-time jobs in the community.

Kids learn valuable lessons from having to contribute to their pursuits in this way. Those who have worked and invested their own money in equipment are more likely to take good care of it, and more likely to value their participation in the sport as well.

Finding Money

Many teams have fundraising activities, too, and it is a good idea to encourage your child's participation as much as possible. In other words, mom and dad shouldn't sell all the candy bars, although it is fine if they help.

Ways that teams can raise money include selling bumper stickers and t-shirts (which also help generate team support), creating media guides or programs and selling ads in those, holding car washes or gift wrapping at a local store, selling discount cards or pizza coupons, selling programs for the school football team, and performing stadium cleanup for a local university sports program.

Be creative with ideas, but make sure the effort will be worth it in terms of the money raised, and that the activity is compatible with the age of the kids and the philosophy of sports and lacrosse. Teams have raised as much as $10,000 or $20,000 from these events when the players and families take them very seriously.

Don't forget to ask former players for their support. The University of California at Berkeley Rugby team is endowed in large part by "Cal Rugby Forever," a 20-year fundraising effort by a group of alumni. This drive funded construction of a field house where team offices and alumni functions are located. A separate group funded construction of the team's home field, Witter Rugby Field, named for the Witter family, which had eleven members play for the Golden Bears. Supporters can make donations to the team through a secure online form. If your team has a website, consider adding this capability.

For large, one-time expenses, consider seeking support from a grandparent or other member of your extended family, or from a community group. Some employers have funds for community outreach and that they might be willing to use to help their employees and their children. It doesn't hurt to ask. This might be appropriate for travel to a tournament or distant camp, for example. If family members provide support, keep the amount at a level that you and your child will feel comfortable with.

Sponsorships

In some sports, sponsorships are sometimes provided by companies, sporting goods manufacturers or other private entities. Before approaching any potential sponsors, develop a proposal that highlights the player's record and includes the following information:

✓ The reason you need a sponsor, including the financial and equipment support and also explaining how this support is going to make a difference in training and development.

✓ Length of time the sponsorship will be required, whether you are looking for support for a one-time need such as a camp, or for a multi-year commitment.

✓ The amount you need, including coaching, equipment, apparel, travel, and entry fees.

✓ What you have to offer a sponsor.

Many individual sponsors expect nothing in return, and sporting goods manufacturers that offer free or discounted equipment do so to generate goodwill and don't expect specific things in return. But a private sponsor is likely to expect the sponsorship to contribute in some way to the company's goals.

For most companies, the marketing or promotions department will be the appropriate contact for requesting sponsorship. Your coach may be able to identify the local representative of a sporting goods manufacturer to receive your proposal.

Parents should be prepared to carefully evaluate any sponsorship opportunities before signing on the dotted line. Consider your player's capabilities and needs and how any possible sponsorship deal helps meets those needs. Pay special attention to:

- The background of the individual sponsor or agent and his reliability going forward.
- The effect of the agreement on any anticipated college scholarships or other plans.
- What the sponsor will expect from the player.
- Contingency clauses and other fine print.

Internships

Many sports marketing organizations offer internships, and some of the top people in these organizations got their start as interns. Most of these internships pay less than a summer job, and some just cover out-of-pocket expenses, but the point of the position is not money. Landing an internship at a top sports company can help a young player appreciate the business side of the sports world, and provide valuable work experience that will broaden future career options.

While many large organizations advertise internship opportunities, smaller companies usually don't, simply because no one has asked them for a position. As a result, these companies may be thrilled to get a call from you. Here are just a few examples of potential sources of sports-related internships:

- Sports marketing, such as IMG (More info: imgworld.com) and Octagon (More info: octagon.com).
- Sports media, such as CNN.
- Endorsement businesses such as Burns Entertainment and Sports Marketing (More info: burnsent.com).
- Sports-related non-profits, such as the Women's Sports Foundation (More info: womenssportsfoundation.org), which also gives grants and scholarships.
- New professional teams and local lacrosse stores.
- Lacrosse organizations such as Inside Lacrosse (More info: insidelacrosse.org) and US Lacrosse (More info: uslacrosse.org).
- Summer camps and local community centers.

Large corporations typically seek out applicants at colleges. The ratio of open positions to applicants can be high, perhaps as much as 1 to 20. Your player will need to put some time and effort into preparing a résumé that highlights playing experience and other assets, and that outlines goals for the future, including how this internship will contribute to meeting those goals.

Plan ahead and use your resources wisely to make lacrosse the most positive experience for your family and your kids. Encourage kids to dream big about lacrosse just as you encourage them to have high hopes in other areas. Then enjoy your role of supporting them - financially and otherwise - in whatever those dreams might be.

Fantasy Lacrosse

Be one of the first to form a team and play in a fantasy lacrosse league. It doesn't cost a thing and won't make you sore. Players can even win sticks, gift certificates, trips to major league games and more. Visit majorleaguelacrosse.com to play.

10

Careers: Where Lacrosse Can Take You

"Lacrosse develops the dynamic work ethic you need to succeed in the business world."
Brad Thawley, Bucknell University midfielder, 2000, and professional financial planner

Kids today can grow up to be just about anything, scientists, restaurant owners, police officers, accountants, musicians, you name it. Kids who are great at lacrosse can also grow up to be professional lacrosse players - or they can turn that talent into a scholarship, major in business or marketing, and become successful entrepreneurs.

As the parent of a lacrosse player, you can rest assured that the sport can play a role in achieving success in any field. The self-discipline, focus, leadership, organizational skills, strategic thinking, physical fitness, and, most importantly, friendships and sense of teamwork that are developed playing lacrosse will be invaluable no matter what path your child ultimately follows.

Defining Career Success

School and career counselors may tell you that kids who develop early career plans are most likely to succeed, and many youngsters today start to weigh career options in high school. But the kids with open minds and attitudes who are interested in exploring many options, and aren't too quick to limit those options, are often the most successful.

Parents and coaches can help kids develop an interest in at least four or five possible career options. As the parent, you will probably want to consider the financial implications of each choice, particularly what it will take financially to prepare for and achieve each option

- and just how much support from you will be appropriate.

The career path children choose can affect just about everything, from how much time they are willing to devote to a specific activity, to what things they read, hobbies and interests, and the people they want to hang out with and even date. Many career planning experts advise their clients to think big and be prepared to adjust their plans as they move forward. As a parent, you can encourage your child to think for himself, too, to make choices based on what will be right for him in the long run - not what his friends are all talking about, what career is the coolest right now, or even what he knows or thinks his parents want.

Any career choice should include a personal definition of success. That definition might include money and fame. But it is important to look around and realize that the people you know who are the most content and who consider themselves most successful are not necessarily - in fact, often not usually - the ones with the most money. And fame seldom brings satisfaction to people who aren't already comfortable with themselves. As John Candy, playing coach Irving Blitzer in the movie "Cool Runnings," said to members of the first Jamaican bobsled team (that's right, bobsled, as in snow and ice), "Gold medals are great. But if you aren't enough without it, you'll never be enough with it."

Over the years, you have probably taught your kids a lot about the importance of friends, family, and community in the personal happiness equation. Keep having those conversations as your child enters and goes through high school - even if it seems like she isn't listening.

Conversations about what's important in life can lead to talking about the role sports can play in a child's future, which can lead to conversations about how sports may lead to a career. Kids who want to make lacrosse, or sports in general, a part of their lives after high school and college have a number of options.

Coaching

Lacrosse is one of the fastest growing sports in the US, and there is a great need for knowledgeable, experienced coaches at all levels - from recreational teams for young kids up through college. US Lacrosse has a comprehensive, multi-level Coaches Education Program online (More info: uslacrosse.org). The organization also has a partnership with the Positive Coaching Alliance, which has a certification program for youth sports and school coaches, also available online (More info: positivecoach.org).

In Canada, there is a competency-based training and certification program operated by the National Coaching Certification Program (NCCP), a partnership between the Coaching Association of Canada (More info: coach.ca); federal, provincial and territorial governments; and more than 60 national sport federations and associations.

Currently in the US, with no certification process, anyone with interest can potentially become a coach. Coaching isn't for everyone, of course; it requires patience, experience, an ability to motivate others and organizational skills in addition to a passion for the game. Players who think they may be interested in coaching can offer to help out with established programs to learn techniques and gain some experience.

School Sports Management

College and high school athletics is a huge segment of the sports industry. Almost every academic institution has an athletic program. About 2,600 high schools have lacrosse teams, and while high school sports management jobs may not be glamorous, the 17,346 high schools that belong to the National Federation of State High Schools (More info: nfhs.org) spend much more on sports programs than the NCAA does. More fans attend high school sports events than collegiate or professional ones. Many sports industry executives started their careers in school athletics.

Coaching a high school lacrosse team is just one of the opportunities available. Most athletic departments have a variety of staff positions, depending on the size of the school and its location, including athletic director, facilities manager, marketing director, development director, and director of student-athlete affairs. Most of these jobs require a degree in liberal arts, education, sports administration or business. Young adults who volunteer or intern with an athletic program can often work their way into a paying job.

Sports Marketing

A career in sports marketing requires a love of sports, first and foremost, along with a bachelor's degree in business, advertising or liberal arts. Solid experience is also a plus. Some of the better-known sports marketing companies include IMG and Octagon. While neither currently represents lacrosse players or teams, it is just a matter of time - and who knows, your kid could be the one to launch the first lacrosse program for a major marketing company!

Sports marketing companies usually focus on three functions: athlete representation, corporate marketing, and event marketing. The Major League Lacrosse (MLL) organization is currently using some of the larger marketing companies to promote its programs.

Athlete Representation

Sports marketing companies negotiate contracts on behalf of professional athletes, and this may be the hard-hitting image that comes to mind when you think of the business. But the companies also provide financial counsel, endorsement marketing, and public relations. Between state requirements and a fiercely competitive world, it can be daunting to break in as a young independent player agent. But there are hundreds of medium to large marketing companies that need talented and eager young recruits.

Corporate Marketing

Agencies develop and execute marketing programs that use sports and sports personalities to promote a company or product. Lacrosse player Kyle Harrison promotes STX products, Warrior Lacrosse has a player's club, and the Powell brothers promote Brine equipment.

Big name athletes often move beyond promoting products related to their sport; for example, cyclist Lance Armstrong has appeared in advertisements for Subaru vehicles, among others, and lacrosse player Mikey Powell has been in ads for Scion. These marketing programs can include simple projects such as sports giveaways up to much grander undertakings such as developing an advertising campaign or having a personality endorse a company's products.

Working for a college athletic department or a local sports team will be good experience from which to launch a sports marketing career. Students can determine what their strengths are and what they enjoy most by exploring various departments, from operations to creative design to management. They should know the players, be familiar with the sports media, be informed about current industry trends, and stay on top of things.

Event Management and Marketing

Managing and marketing major sports events like the International Lacrosse Federation (ILF) World Championships, NCAA Championships, and even National All-Star Games require considerable experience and expertise. These events take a lot of money and a large team of people to produce. A typical event team includes an event director, marketing director, facilities manager, sales director, director of operations and client services coordinator.

The event director oversees the entire event, works to secure sponsorships from corporations, and signs up teams. The sales manager sells advertising space in printed material, the venue and other outlets, and coordinates promotional campaigns and ticket sales. The client services coordinator responds to the needs of sponsors, advertisers and teams, and oversees corporate ticket sales. The marketing director coordinates advertising and promotion in advance of the event.

Canadian Championship Events

Teams at various levels in Canada vie for a number of championship trophies. The Minto Cup is given to the national champion at the Junior A level each year, and the Founders Trophy to the national champs at the Junior B level. The President's Cup goes to the national box lacrosse champions at the Senior B level. Senior men's field teams compete for the P.D. Ross Cup and Victory Trophy, and Junior men's field teams compete for the First Nations Trophy. The Mann Cup, one of the most important trophies in Canada, goes to the champion from the Ontario Lacrosse Association and Western Lacrosse Association box major league series.

Lacrosse Officiating

Has your kid always wanted to get back at those players who kept throwing illegal checks? Then lacrosse officiating is for him. Just kidding, of course. But there are good reasons for an interest in officiating.

Working as a lacrosse referee is not a full-time job, but is a great way to stay connected to the game, earn a little money, and enjoy being the authority on the field. If that last part doesn't appeal to you, you probably aren't referee material. Every college game ideally has three referees, the head official, field judge and line judge. High school games usually have two officials, and many youth games use only one. Still, there are plenty of opportunities

to officiate at a variety of levels, between regular season games, tournament games, camp games, and exhibitions. To get started, a would-be referee must pass a written test. In the US, this is given by US Lacrosse (More info: lacrosse.org).

The Canadian Lacrosse Association (More info: lacrosse.ca) administers testing for referees in that country. Officials can work their way up from high school games to the college level, and can also officiate professional games.

Pay is determined by level, with NCAA refs making $125 to $200 per game. The days can be long and hard, but the sense of satisfaction from officiating a tough, close game can only be fully understood and felt by those who have done it. There is also the satisfaction of giving back to lacrosse. There is a shortage of experienced, quality officials and the game needs good officials, especially those who have played the game.

Athletic Trainer

An athletic trainer works to keep players in top physical condition and prevent injuries. When a player is hurt, it is the trainer's job to design a treatment program and oversee rehabilitation. This position is also called physical conditioning trainer, strength and conditioning trainer, and personal fitness trainer, although the latter not so much in a team sport like lacrosse.

The American Medical Association recognizes trainers as allied health professionals. The National Athletic Trainers Association (NATA; More info: nata.org) is the main certifying organization for trainers. A bachelor's degree, at minimum, is required, and completion of a program in athletic training.

NATA also requires a passing score on a multi-part examination and hundreds of hours of supervised experience, usually working with head trainers at colleges. Many states require trainers to be registered or licensed.

Most of the trainer jobs are at colleges and high schools. Health clubs, large corporations, and lacrosse organizations also hire athletic trainers. The best-paying jobs will be at the professional level, but these positions are also the hardest to get. A great way to get started here, too, is by volunteering or working part-time while still in school.

Trainers may find membership in the National Strength and Conditioning Association useful (More info: nsca-lift.org). The people in this profession provide an invaluable service to all athletic teams and have become more common at all levels of the lacrosse scene in recent years.

Sports Entrepreneur

A star lacrosse player at Princeton, David Morrow was a 1992 and 1993 All-American, 1993 Defenseman of the Year, and NCAA Most Valuable Player in Division I Lacrosse. He competed for Team USA in 1994 and 1998, when the team won World Championships. In 1993, he founded Warrior Lacrosse Inc, which has become one of the leading providers of innovative and high performance lacrosse equipment in the world.

Now serving as the company CEO and chairman, Morrow also sponsors professional and intercollegiate teams as well as more than 200 youth programs and camps each year, and was a founding partner of MLL. He used his experience as a player and relationships in the industry to launch the company, which allows him to promote the game and make a living while he's at it.

Many compare lacrosse in the US today to where soccer was ten years ago. The sport's exploding popularity creates a lot of opportunities. It can also create some problems; too many people wanting to "cash in" on the boom. Certainly, more people are going to be able to make a living in some way that is related to lacrosse, but would-be entrepreneurs would be well advised to proceed with caution.

Don't jump at any opportunity without thoroughly checking out the other people involved, and being realistic about the prospects. Still, for a talented and hard-working young person with a good idea and a solid education, sports entrepreneurship can lead to dreams come true.

Sports Media

Sports-related media have come a long way from the newspaper sports page and a few minutes on the evening television news. Now there are entire television networks, internet sites, glossy magazines like *Inside Lacrosse*, and a proliferation of sports talk radio shows.

There are even a few weekly lacrosse television shows. The MLL is on ESPN, Fox Sports Network and Comcast in local regions. Johns Hopkins University signed a deal with ESPNU to broadcast all home men's lacrosse games through 2009, and College Sports Television gave Navy an exclusive deal for its home games. Syracuse has a deal locally with Time Warner to televise games.

Every spring, there are more and more lacrosse games broadcast on television. In short, the opportunities to work in sports media are many.

A print publication or sports website typically has a team that includes editors, writers, photographers, designers, advertising sales and promotions. At radio and television shows, there are also hosts, producers, engineers and technical production staff. Most of the specialized jobs require a degree in journalism or a related field. Internships can be a great way to break in.

Successful athletes can often find their way into broadcasting because of their name recognition and knowledge of sports. A willingness to learn about the business and thorough preparation are important if this move is to succeed.

When to Turn Pro

The time for a young player to turn professional in lacrosse is after college graduation. There are two professional leagues in the US and Canada, and it is doubtful any of the players on teams in either earn enough solely from playing to live on. Most players have other jobs, some in the lacrosse industry.

If your kid is interested in someday turning pro, go ahead and encourage and support that. But keep a realistic perspective on the extremely low odds of him making a pro team (and there are currently no women's professional teams), and make sure he understands what it will take to make it.

Those new to professional sports are often surprised by the vast difference between high school and even college competition and the professional level. Your role as parent is to help your kid, along with his coach, assess his ability and drive for this highest level. A player must exhibit consistent performance at a high level of competition before he is ready to go pro.

At the professional level, success is more dependent on ability than effort, although it takes plenty of that, too. As the parent, you can also help your kid determine what his options are for a job compatible with the team's schedule. This would be a good time to review some of the important lessons you've been teaching him as he has grown - about budgeting, saving and making wise choices with his money.

There is a draft each year at the end of the college season and many graduating players are scooped up by Major League Lacrosse and, later, the National Lacrosse League. As the league expands, more opportunities will open up for players. Several new teams have started in the West, creating many playing opportunities.

More and more players are taking advantage of professional representation, hiring an agent to represent them in negotiations with teams. For a solid, talented player, an agent can mean a better contract and good advice on other matters. But lacrosse is not yet to the point where every player needs an agent.

Would-be pros will simply need to look at the pros and cons for their individual situation and decide accordingly. Agents can be hired through the NLL Professional Lacrosse Players Association (More info: plpa.com) and other organizations.

Most people choose a career based on what they enjoy, and lacrosse can serve as a springboard to many places. A kid who grows up staying connected to the game, doing what he loves and making a living at it is a lucky kid indeed. And so are his parents!

Post-College Lacrosse for Women

Some lacrosse players parlay their experience into a career, or at least put skills learned on the field to use in their working life. Many also continue to play the game wherever and whenever they can. Individuals are sometimes able to seek out a team, but sometimes, players have to create a team themselves.

The Men's Division of US Lacrosse has had organized lacrosse leagues since 1998. Now, the Women's Division Post-Collegiate Club has been launched by US Lacrosse to create an outlet for female lacrosse players to connect and grow leagues and clubs for those who want to continue playing after college (More info: uslacrosse.org).

The organization's website helps women who want to start a new team, to connect players in the same areas and across the country, and provides up-to-date information on tournaments and regulations. There are about 50 post-collegiate club teams around the country, but many are unaware of other nearby teams, or of opportunities to compete nationally.

The Women's Division Post-Collegiate Club has a directory of team contacts, produces an electronic newsletter, and distributes brochures at tournaments and other events to spread the word. The "Post-Collegiate Start-Up Manual" provides tips and insights on starting a club.

One team in Arizona - far from any of the country's established lacrosse communities - holds practices and scrimmages, and plays against teams at the University of Arizona and Arizona State. Players are even starting to coach high school teams - passing on the love of the game to a new generation. Some of them will, no doubt, one day be playing post-collegiate lacrosse.

11

Building A Lacrosse Community

"Never doubt that a small group of thoughtful, committed citizens can change the world. Indeed, it is the only thing that ever has."
Margaret Mead, world-renowned anthropologist

While lacrosse is catching on big time across the country and around the world, maybe the craze has yet to reach your community. You have no teams, no players, and all the wide grassy fields are covered with football or soccer players. What's a wanna-be lacrosse star to do? Well, start the ball rolling yourself.

US Lacrosse

If you're a coach or a player, you may already belong to US Lacrosse (More info: uslacrosse.org), a non-profit organization founded in 1990 as the national governing body for men's and women's lacrosse in the U.S.

For parents and kids new to lacrosse, this can be a good place to start. The organization has a New Start Program for first-year teams at any level. They will guide you through recruiting coaches and officials, provide rule books and parent's guides, and offer a one-time discount on equipment through participating manufacturers. You can also apply for start-up grants to buy goals, balls, and other equipment. More than 54 local and regional chapters make contact easy.

Working with Parks and Recreation

Lacrosse programs can be run on public fields, including city soccer complexes and parks, public school fields, private school facilities and other venues. The key is getting permission from the appropriate authority and abiding by rules - and inviting the owners, operators or users of those facilities to come out and watch a lacrosse game. Field space can often be a limiting factor, so it is important to develop good relationships with field supervisors and athletic directors.

Find out what, if any, lacrosse programs exist in your area. There may be school teams, clubs, recreational leagues or even a college team. Search on the internet, call the parks and recreation department and the school district. Find out how the programs are funded. Local tax dollars usually fund community facilities, for example. Other organizations may be dues supported. Identify whether these programs meet your particular need, be that a team for beginning players, players not affiliated with a particular school, or those needing more challenging levels of competition. Talk to existing programs about the possibility of expanding to address your need, if necessary, or organize other families in starting a new program.

One great way to generate interest in the community is to bring in a professional lacrosse player to run a clinic. You can seek a grant or sponsorship to pay the player's and other expenses and offer the clinic for free, or charge a nominal amount, say $10 per participant, to cover some of your costs. Players at the professional level of a sport are a big draw for kids (and their parents!) and in most cases are very approachable and interested in supporting the sport.

Developing Lacrosse Facilities

If there aren't enough fields in your area, or the availability is limited, you can lead the drive to create more fields or to open up existing fields to lacrosse. Access to a place to play and exposure to games will draw many kids to the sport.

Contact all the groups and organizations in the area with a vested interest in developing lacrosse facilities - recreational leagues, school teams, club teams, coaches, the parks and recreation department, health organizations and local sports-related businesses. Remind them of the statistics on overweight youth and the importance of physical exercise. Based on the support you receive, and the spaces potentially available, decide whether your field will be a public, private or club facility.

A private landowner, for example, or a subdivision, may provide land for a field, with use restricted to a specific club or team, or residents of the neighborhood. If the parks and recreation department has a place for a field, that will be one open to anyone in the city. Some facilities are partnerships between various entities, such as the city and a club, with wider access than a private facility but some restrictions.

Fortunately, a lacrosse field is not a high-end development. You need adequate space, level and well-drained land, and access. The minimum space needed for a field is 110 yards by 70 yards wide, with roughly ten yards on either side for the teams and fans. Many football and soccer fields work well, with some additional lining. Beyond that, your club, team or volunteers can put in grass, a sprinkler system and options like a storage facility, bleachers or a scoreboard. Lacrosse goals can be moved after each game and practice and stored in a relatively small space - including the garage of a lacrosse parent. This is a plus where lacrosse shares field space with other sports.

Developing Volunteers

Volunteers will be the backbone of your lacrosse community. Fortunately, volunteering can easily fit into busy lives and can actually enhance your family together time and quality of life.

The entire family can turn out to prepare fields, watch a game, serve refreshments at half-time, and collect the money from the team's latest fundraising effort. You all get to spend time together, enjoy exciting entertainment, get to know some new friends and generally share a good time.

Recruiting Volunteers

Recruiting volunteers and keeping them motivated is an important role of a community lacrosse association, whether it is a recreational league, school booster club, or club team. People volunteer for a variety of reasons, including a desire to feel needed, share a skill, get to know others in the community, learn something new, gain recognition, explore a career, gain status, or simply enjoy some free time.

For you parents, it's a great way to become involved with your kids. Bottom line, though, volunteers want to enjoy what they are doing and work for a cause they care about. Offer your volunteers jobs they will enjoy doing and where they can see their contribution, and remember to recognize them for that contribution on a regular basis. This doesn't have to be a big deal, a simple thank you is often enough.

Parents of players will be your number one source of volunteers. Some other places to find volunteers:

✓ Schools. Contact the principal, athletic director or parent association. At the high school level, many students need volunteer hours for honor societies and other organizations.
✓ Colleges. Contact the dean of students. Again, students may have volunteer requirements.
✓ Churches and temples. Contact the pastor, rabbi or priest.
✓ Professional associations. Like those for lawyers, tax advisors, bookkeepers. Contact presidents of associations.
✓ Veterans' organizations. VFW, AMVETS, American Legion and similar veterans' organizations sometimes have buildings available for team meetings and parties, and even fields.
✓ Social and business organizations, like Rotary, Optimist and Lions Clubs. These groups will particularly want to help if your programs include efforts to offer the lacrosse experience to kids who might not otherwise get it.
✓ Special interest groups like photography clubs, sports groups and hobby organizations.

Training Volunteers

Once you've recruited the volunteers, provide them with any training and encouragement necessary for the jobs you are asking them to do. This might be as simple as having an experienced time-keeper sit with a new volunteer through several games until the rookie feels comfortable with the job, or as involved as sending volunteers to a training session for officials or coaches.

The first time working a game can be hectic with coaches and officials demanding information, and a trained volunteer will likely feel more confident and comfortable. Contact US Lacrosse or a local lacrosse organization to find out about training opportunities for officials, coaches and players. This can be an opportunity for parents to learn more about the game, too. There are jobs for everyone - parents can help clean up after games, provide snacks, collect dues, take pictures and, of course, cheer for the team, without any training.

Developing Lacrosse Coaches

Coaches in your area may be glad to have additional opportunities to make a little more money since many club teams pay only a small stipend to coaches, and rec league coaches are typically volunteers. To keep up a coach's enthusiasm, team parents can provide a financial thank you at the end of the season. Coaches are often also eager to help develop younger players who can move up onto their existing team. Ask if your experienced coach will put on a workshop for volunteer coaches. US Lacrosse has a Coaches Education Program and partners with the Positive Coaching Alliance, and even offers grants for training sessions. Some city parks and recreation departments offer similar training. Some even require certain training for their volunteer coaches, a response to increasing incidents of conflict at sports events.

Funding Your Efforts

Launching lacrosse in your area, or significantly boosting participation in an existing program, takes money, just like any new venture. An important part of your efforts will be finding and developing funding sources, which will mean putting on an impressive presentation, asking for support, and following up.

If you are passionate about lacrosse - and you probably are if you're at this point - this should be relatively easy. Fortunately, you won't need a huge amount of money to get started. But keep the long-term picture in mind and recruit folks with fundraising experience for your organization so you will have the ability to grow the program.

Support from Organizations

The US Lacrosse Building Relationships to Initiate Diversity, Growth and Enrichment (BRIDGE) initiative works to expand the game in non-traditional and underserved communities across the nation. It also has equipment grants and a New Start Program for first-year teams or programs at all levels.

Don't limit your search to lacrosse organizations, though. More than 70,000 foundations nationwide offer grants to non-profit organizations (More info: fdncenter.org). Incorporating local, non-lacrosse issues into your program will greatly increase your options. Consider how your efforts will improve physical fitness of the youth in your community, offer them productive activities (anti-drug and anti-crime money, anyone?), create more open space, encourage family time, promote the participation of girls in team sports - the possibilities are many. Ask for support from groups working on particular issues, such as the Women's Sports Foundation's Community Action Program (More info: womenssportsfoundation.org).

In-kind Support

Donations of products and services can be just as valuable as money; anything you don't have to rent or buy saves your cash for other things. Here are a few possibilities:

- Field use from parks and recreation, a school or other entity.
- Balls, jerseys, goals, and other equipment and supplies. Talk with your US Lacrosse chapter, a lacrosse manufacturer, or a local sporting goods store.
- Help with promotional materials and publicity.
- Professional services such as legal, tax, or sprinkler maintenance.

- Meeting rooms.
- Instruction by local coaches or trainers.
- Local restaurants, pizza shops, ice cream shops, water bottlers.

Fundraising

A special event can put some green stuff in your coffers. An afternoon car wash, lacrosse clinic, or formal awards banquet can all work. Just consider your community's culture and interests, and your potential audience.

If you live in a laid-back surfer community, skip the formal dinner and have a barbecue on the beach. But if everyone else is having cook-outs, tap into an unmet need for that fancy-dress evening. Lacrosse players clean up pretty well!

Scholastic Lacrosse

Roughly 134,000 boys and girls played on high school lacrosse teams in 2004 - and that number is growing every year, with data from the National Federation of State High School Associations showing lacrosse as the fastest growing of any high school sport in the previous ten years.

High school players may also qualify for league, regional and state championships operated by the state athletic association. If your area schools don't have lacrosse, contact US Lacrosse about starting a team, and to help determine whether a school-sponsored or club team will be best for your needs.

Publicity

You need to get the word out but probably don't have a huge media budget. There are plenty of cheap but effective ways to generate publicity. Tap into the talent among your players and parents to develop your materials, or use those already available, such as a promotional video and Power Point presentation provided by US Lacrosse. Part of the organization's mission is to promote the sport, so you are helping them as well.

Here are some tried and true ideas:

- ✓ Put up flyers and posters at area schools and gathering places like coffee shops, ice cream and pizza parlors, recreational facilities and sporting goods stores. Make yard signs for all your players, and post these on strategic corners of your target neighborhoods. Be sure to put some up around the fields, where active types will see them. Pass out flyers at other sporting events.
- ✓ Bring in a lacrosse pro or a local college star player to conduct a clinic, hold a demonstration for your kid's gym class, or to sign autographs at a game.
- ✓ Send notices to local newspapers, neighborhood newsletters, and other publications for their community calendars. If you have great action shots of lacrosse, provide copies to the publications that use photos.
- ✓ Don't forget the reach and power of the Internet. Create a website for your league or team that lists upcoming games and events and lets people know how they can support you. Register your site with leading directories like Yahoo. Always include your web address on flyers and other materials.
- ✓ Look for human interest angles that the media will be intrigued by - the team that cleaned up a down-and-out park to create playing space, the coach who recruited a couple of troubled kids who turned themselves around.

Creating a Tournament or Event

Kids love a little competition, if the setting is friendly and the emphasis is on fun, and not on winning or losing. Organizing a lacrosse tournament or fun event can help increase the visibility of the sport in your area, attract potential players and perhaps even generate a little income for your team or league. You'll need a place to play, sponsors to cover your major expenses, players, and, of

The Dream of Playing Lacrosse

Lacrosse has motivated many a youngster to work harder in school, or to stay in shape. It has even been the reason some kids stay out of trouble. For one young athlete in Austin, Texas, lacrosse is part of the dream of a normal future that keeps her going. Megan Horton, born with a serious heart condition, was told that her only option was a heart transplant.

While waiting for a heart to become available, she has fallen in love with lacrosse. Her big brother Ryan plays for the Westwood High School Warriors lacrosse team and Megan makes nearly every game, encouraging the players, watching the action, supporting the team. The players, who all treat her like a little sister, say she is an inspiration to them. And with Westwood starting a girls' lacrosse program, Megan is hoping that she'll soon be able to leave the sidelines and take her place on the field.

course, publicity - but by now you're just about an expert at all those things.

Find your players at schools, in recreational leagues and on club teams, and at local camps. You'll need a minimum of four to six teams of at least 15 players each. This may be a good way to match individual players with a team, if you have some unattached folks show up. Teams should be more or less evenly matched; you want everyone to feel challenged, but don't want anyone to be humiliated or turned off from the sport. Coaches of established teams should know whether participating teams are good matches. If the goal is playing time and fun for all, consider mixing players up to create special teams just for the tournament, putting a few of the best players on each team along with less experienced ones.

Choose an appropriate format, which might be double elimination, every team plays two games, or another standard tournament format. This will depend partly on how many teams you have and the goals of your event.

Emphasize the fun factor by giving awards for most improved players, good sportsmanship, and play of the game. Have off-the-field activities like a "moonwalk" for younger kids, skills games - shooting at targets with a lacrosse stick and ball, dunk the coach - and refreshments. Selling these for a nominal fee can raise additional funds - just stick with mostly healthy stuff. This could be a good opportunity to recognize your volunteers, too.

Let players support their lacrosse community by working a shift at an activity booth or refreshment table, lining fields for play, officiating for younger teams, and picking up after the event.

Building a Business

If you're the entrepreneurial type or want to make profitable use of your free time, start a business that develops lacrosse programs for kids. Developing recreational players can be a fun experience and a potential business opportunity. Start small, and pool your resources - a parent, coach and business person can build a viable business.

The ultimate goal is to have more kids playing more lacrosse, and having fun doing it. There are lots of ways to help make this happen, and coaches and parents working together can be the driving force behind bringing the game to every community.

12

The Lacrosse World And Beyond

"Convincing fans that lacrosse is an exciting game is no problem, and the momentum is building. But lacrosse still has a long way to go."
Adam Miner, CPA, MLL Project Leader and AEG Marketing, Los Angeles Riptide

There are all kinds of people involved in lacrosse, and all kinds of entities organizing, promoting and developing the sport. As parents and coaches, if we can tap into the right organizations and services, we can do a better job of helping our kids make the most of their lacrosse experience. We can also do our part to help grow the sport in all its different venues.

US Lacrosse

US Lacrosse (More info: uslacrosse.org) is the central governing body for men's and women's lacrosse in the United States. More than 200,000 players, coaches, officials and fans are members of the organization, which has the stated mission to promote and develop the sport. It puts on the Intercollegiate Associates National Championships, the championship for college lacrosse.

Lacrosse Intercollegiate Associates includes roughly 185 men's and 170 women's college teams, which are not varsity sports at their schools but follow similar guidelines and compete at a more organized level than club programs. US Lacrosse also runs the Women's Divisions National Tournament (the club lacrosse championship), National Youth Festivals, and High School Showcases. These events generate much of the organization's revenues. The website has rules of the game, science and safety, education and training info, tips on starting a team, lacrosse news, and coaching jobs.

Annual membership is $20 for youth players (under age 15 and not in high school); $35 for high school players and assistant/youth/club and junior volunteer coaches; and $50 for adult players, head coaches and officials. Membership includes a monthly magazine, insurance coverage, membership in a local chapter, a monthly email newsletter, discounts, free admission to the Lacrosse Museum and Hall of Fame, and eligibility to participate in US Lacrosse events. Fan memberships are $40 and include all benefits except insurance. Membership also supports the organization and all of its programs. There are additional opportunities to get involved, including volunteering at local events, serving in a local chapter or participating on organization committees.

US Lacrosse employs a staff of about 40 at its national headquarters in Baltimore, MD. The organization is run by a national board of directors, over divisions for men's and women's lacrosse, with councils representing the various constituencies and committees that focus on specific areas of operation. Many volunteers in these and other positions help the organization function.

There are 54 regional chapters of US Lacrosse throughout the country. These affiliates of the national organization receive a portion of the membership dues. The chapters unify the local lacrosse community, provide services in the area, and serve as a central source of information, programs and events. Find your local chapter on the website.

Canadian Lacrosse

The Canadian Lacrosse Association (More info: lacrosse.ca) is the governing body for Canadian lacrosse and is committed to enhancing the growth and development of country's national summer sport. It sponsors the World Men's Field Lacrosse Championships.

The website has the philosophy and history of the sport, information for coaches and officials, information on box lacrosse and men's and women's field lacrosse, team rosters, and events. The association also operates the Canadian Lacrosse Hall of Fame in New Westminster, Canada.

NFHS

In the United States, principals, superintendents and school boards at most junior high and high schools belong to the state school athletic association. The association, also called a federation, sets rules for high school athletics in the particular state, controls athlete recruiting, holds championships and otherwise governs school sports.

These associations are, in turn, members of a national organization, the National Federation of State High School Associations (More info: nfhs.org). This body provides leadership and national coordination for the state school athletic associations. NFHS also publishes reports on sports safety issues and tracks participation levels in various school sports. State associations in NFHS represent 17,346 high schools and roughly 10 million students involved in high school programs, and publish playing rules in 16 sports, including boy's and girl's lacrosse.

In many states, such as Texas, lacrosse is still a club sport, not a school sport. Club teams use published rules from the NCAA rulebook, with certain adaptations for high school. Some communities adopt rule changes specifically for their leagues concerning things like grades the players must maintain, penalties for fighting and so forth.

Lacrosse Camps

There are hundreds of camps all across the country and the numbers keep growing. These camps are offered by colleges and universities with lacrosse programs; major lacrosse manufacturers like Warrior, Brine and STX (More info: allaboutlax.com). Organizations like Adrenaline Lacrosse and MVP Lacrosse also offer camps, often led by college players and coaches. You can also find lacrosse programs hosted at youth and general sports camps. *Lacrosse Magazine*'s March issue lists most camps in the US.

NCAA

The National Collegiate Athletic Association (More info: ncaa.org), whose members include colleges, universities and conferences, exists to govern competition in a fair, safe, equitable and sportsmanlike manner, and to integrate intercollegiate athletics into higher education. The organization provides financial assistance and other help to groups to promote and advance intercollegiate athletics, compiles statistics, and keeps regular season and championship records.

NCAA also promotes all intercollegiate athletics and 88 championship events in 23 sports, including the college championships for men's and women's lacrosse. NCAA operations are run by an executive committee made up of representatives from schools in each division, with many committees under the executive one. There are rules committees for men's and for women's lacrosse, and committees for men's and women's lacrosse at each Division. Season records determine team spots in the playoffs for the NCAA Championship game each May.

NCAA schools are classified into one of three divisions, based on how many sports are offered at the school and the availability of athletic scholarships. The classification has no relation to a school's reputation or other qualities. Division I institutions sponsor at least seven sports for men and seven for women, with two team sports for each gender, and must play all of the minimum number of games against Division I opponents, and meet some minimum attendance requirements. Division I schools have minimum financial aid requirements as well.

Schools in Division II have to sponsor at least four sports, including two team sports, for men and for women, with contest and participation minimums for each. Division III schools must sponsor at least five sports each for men and women, with two team sports. There are about 221 men's lacrosse and 175 women's lacrosse teams at the college level in all three divisions. The opportunities in women's lacrosse have increased greatly in recent years, while the growth in men's lacrosse has slowed somewhat, a function in part of Title IX, which deals with gender equity in college athletics.

Because of the relative size of athletic budgets, many of the best coaches and players are at Division I schools, and these are typically the best teams. Division II and III teams play quality lacrosse that is challenging for participants and plenty exciting for spectators, though.

NAIA

The National Association of Intercollegiate Athletics is the second-largest association of accredited four-year college sports. The NAIA does not include lacrosse programs.

NJCAA

Junior colleges offer another level of opportunity for students who want to play lacrosse, but who aren't sure if they want to attend a four-year college. The National Junior College Athletic Association (More info: njcaa.org) has 26 member institutions offering men's lacrosse, and 12 offering women's lacrosse. The organization hosts the annual Men's Invitational Lacrosse Championships and Women's Invitational Lacrosse Championships. Many star players in Divisions I, II and III got their start on junior college teams.

Tournaments

In addition to all the tournaments sponsored by the organizations mentioned in this chapter, there are dozens and dozens of fun tournaments in places like Hawaii, Sonoma, Vail and Lake Tahoe, sponsored by US Lacrosse, manufacturers, and organizations, usually made up of lacrosse players and enthusiasts who want to play and watch more lacrosse. You can find these events on lacrosse-related websites and in lacrosse magazines, as well as in local publications and on community calendars. If there isn't one in your area, maybe it's time you started one!

Levels start at youth and go all the way up to the super masters, for the old guys who still want to swing a stick.

World Indoor Lacrosse Championship

The International Lacrosse Federation (More info: worldindoorlacrosse.com) sponsors the annual world professional indoor championship tournament and holds a series of other events.

World Lacrosse Events

The International Lacrosse Federation World Championship tournament features more than 20 teams from all over the world vying for bragging rights as the world's lacrosse powerhouse.

The International Federation of Women's Lacrosse Associations holds a World Cup championship game every few years (More info: uslacrosse.org). Over ten nations participate including Australia, United States, England and Canada.

Blue Flag Rule at Amsterdam Tournament

Lacrosse buffs have held several tournaments in Amsterdam, with roughly 16 men's and 16 women's teams participating, to fuel enthusiasm for the sport in Europe.

The events are hosted by Maastricht Lacrosse, a club team representing Maastricht University and the first lacrosse team in the Netherlands, with support from Euro-Lax, a manufacturer and distributor of lacrosse equipment in Europe. Entry fees paid for use of fields and clubhouse, locker and shower rooms, referees, administration, clean-up, and, of course, a post-tourney party.

In keeping with the goal of having fun and enjoying the game, the tournament applied the "Geen Gezeik" rule, enforced by a blue flag. Geen Gezeik means, essentially, "no carping" in Dutch. Referees have a no-tolerance policy on complaining about calls, which applies to coaches and players. First offense is a one-minute penalty. Second offense by the same person results in suspension to the beer tent for attitude adjustment for the remainder of the game.

This "time out" for adults was well-received at the tournaments. Europeans almost never yell at officials, while it has become common practice in the US and Canada. Perhaps the Blue Flag idea will catch on elsewhere. Give it a try at your event for the adults!

Professional Lacrosse Player's Association

Players in the National Lacrosse League can join The Professional Lacrosse Player's Association (More info: plpa.com), which represents the player's interests and promotes professional lacrosse. The website includes upcoming events, player rosters and stats, tips from pro players, merchandise and news.

National Lacrosse League

The National Lacrosse League (NLL; More info: nll.com) is North America's professional indoor lacrosse league, with 11 professional teams in two divisions, East and West. The teams are:

- ❖ Arizona Sting
- ❖ Buffalo (NY) Bandits
- ❖ Calgary (Canada) Roughnecks
- ❖ Colorado Mammoth
- ❖ Edmonton (Canada) Rush
- ❖ Minnesota Swarm
- ❖ Philadelphia Wings
- ❖ Portland Lumberjax
- ❖ Rochester Knighthawks
- ❖ San Jose Stealth
- ❖ Toronto Rock

A new franchise in Chicago, the Shamrox, and a New York team joined the league for the 2007 season. The season runs December through April, followed by the Champion's Cup Playoffs. Indoor lacrosse differs somewhat from field lacrosse. Check those differences out under Lax 101 on the NLL website.

Major League Lacrosse

Founded in 2001, a new franchise, Major League Lacrosse (MLL) has ten teams divided into Eastern and Western Divisions:

❖ Baltimore Bayhawks
❖ Boston Cannons
❖ Long Island Lizards
❖ New Jersey Pride
❖ Philadelphia Barrage
❖ Rochester Rattlers
❖ Chicago Machine
❖ Denver Outlaws
❖ Los Angeles Riptide
❖ San Francisco Dragons

For more information about teams and their schedules go to: majorleaguelacrosse.com. MLL's season runs from May through August plus special events including the Warrior Major League Challenge in May, All Star Game in July, and the New Balance Major League Lacrosse Championship Weekend in August. The website, majorleaguelacrosse.com includes team rosters and stats; news; game schedules; information on events like drafts, championships and all-star games; photos and video highlights; and even job listings.

The history and growth of the sport have been very different on the two coasts of the US. On the East Coast, there is tremendous familiarity with the sport and a solid fan base. But most are devoted to NCAA lacrosse and to particular college teams. Fans don't typically follow their favorite players from college to pro teams, as they do in many other sports. The MLL and NLL are working hard to change that and to find other ways to move fans to professional lacrosse.

Lacrosse is less well-established on the West Coast. Here, professional teams are more entrepreneurial ventures and must work to build their markets. Lacrosse has several positive marketing messages: it is one of the least expensive sporting events around, offers a great atmosphere to promote values, and is entertaining on a number of levels. It's affordable, family-friendly fun.

International Lacrosse

There are lacrosse leagues, teams and annual tournaments literally around the world, including Australia, New Zealand, Germany, Czechoslovakia, England, Wales, Japan, Hong Kong, and Argentina. Links to many of their websites are available at lacrosse.ca.

Coaches Organizations

US Lacrosse has a Men's Division Coaches Council and the Women's Division Coaches Council, with subcommittees for high school and college, which provide education, guidelines and other support.

The Positive Coaching Alliance (More info: positivecoach.org) provides training and certification for youth coaches and tools such as a parent letter and parent pledge, positive charting and coaching scripts.

Individual collegiate coaches can belong to the Intercollegiate Men's Lacrosse Coaches Association (More info: lacrossecoaches.stcnetsite.com), created to help build the game of lacrosse by providing coach development and monitoring the integrity of the game. The organization holds an annual coaching clinic. The Intercollegiate Women's Lacrosse Coaches Association (More info: iwlca.org) is a non-profit organization for coaches from Divisions I, II and III, dedicated to promoting the game and to the education of its coaches.

Hall of Fame

There are several places where you can be inspired by the best players lacrosse has to offer: The US Lacrosse Museum and Hall of Fame in Baltimore, Maryland; Canadian Hall of Fame in New Westminster, British Columbia; and the NCAA Hall of Fame, which features all NCAA sports, including lacrosse.

It doesn't matter whether players dream of the Hall of Fame, college glory, professional play, or just pretend to score the winning goal with two seconds left on the clock. We hope everyone has a great time playing or supporting lacrosse. After all, it's simply the fastest, most creative and most fun game on two feet.

Select References

Bob Bigelow, Tom Moroney, Linda Hall, *Just Let the Kids Play*, HCI, 2001

Donald M. Fisher, *Lacrosse: A History of the Game*, Johns Hopkins University Press, 2002

Fred Engh, *Why Johnny Hates Sports*, Square One, 2002

Jordan Metzl, M.D., Carol Shookhoff, *The Young Athlete: A Sports Doctor's Complete Guide for Parents*, Little Brown, 2003

Lacrosse Magazine, *Lacrosse: North America's Game*, Carpenter, 2004

Credits

- Front Cover Photo of Daniel Castelline by permission of Nancy Castelline.
- Front Cover Photo of Antonio Carlos Aleman by permission of Joy Aleman.
- Back Cover Photo by permission of Jeff Nutt.
- Attributions to Patrick Gowan by permission of Patrick Gowan.
- Leah Dubie quote by permission of Leah Dubie.
- Attributions to Kim Coffey by permission of Kim Coffey.
- Attributions to Jordan Metzl, MD., from The Young Athlete. Reprinted by permission of Jordan Metzl.
- Tal Alter attributions by permission of Tal Alter.
- Attributions to Fred Engh from Why Johnny Hates Sports. Reprinted by permission of Fred Engh.
- Alex Cade quote by permission of Alex Cade.
- Scott Hochstadt quote by permission of Scott Hochstadt.
- Brian Ferry quote by permission of Brian Ferry.
- Justin Smith quote by permission of Justin Smith.
- Attributions to Andrew Combs by permission of Andrew Combs.
- Attributions to Ricky Sowell by permission of Ricky Sowell.
- Ernst Leiss quote by permission of Ernst Leiss.
- Brad Thawley quote by permission of Brad Thawley.
- Adam Miner quote by permission of Adam Miner.
- Margaret Mead quote by permission of The Institute of Intercultural Studies, Inc.

Index

Interval training, 50, 51

L

Learning about Lacrosse, 4
Line drills, 47

M

Major League Lacrosse, 1, 13, 4,
    29, 70, 118, 125, 149
Mental conditioning, 52
MLL, 70, 118, 123, 124, 149

N

NATA, 122
National Athletic Trainers
    Association, 122
National Collegiate Athletic
    Association, 96, 144
National Federation of State High
    School Associations, 99, 136,
    143
National Junior College Athletic
    Association, 145
National Lacrosse League, 4, 12,
    125, 148
National Strength and
    Conditioning Association, 123
NCAA, 3, 66, 70, 96, 98, 99, 100,
    101, 102, 103, 104, 105, 117, 119,
    122, 123, 143, 144, 149, 152
NFHS, 143
NJCAA, 145
NLL, 125, 148, 149

P

Pain
    bad pain, 25, 58, 59
    good pain, 25, 58, 59

Parent as Coach, 34
Participation in other sports, 54
Plyometrics, 51
Positive Coaching Alliance, 33,
    117, 151
practice, 159
Process versus Outcome Goals, 66
Publicity, 136

R

Read Up, 6
roadmap, 159

S

Scholastic Lacrosse, 136
Sponsorships, 111

T

Two on One Ground Balls, 47

U

US Lacrosse, 104, 113, 117, 122,
    127, 129, 133, 135, 136, 141, 142,
    146, 151, 152

V

Volunteers, 131, 132, 133

W

Watch a Camp Session, 5
Why Lacrosse?, 3
World Indoor Lacrosse
    Championship, 146
World Lacrosse Events, 146

Get More!

Sizzle Up Your Next Lacrosse Event:

Contact Noah and Melissa, and discover new ways how they can support your lacrosse team, fund-raiser, club and community.

Contact

Noah Fink: noah@mansiongrovehouse.com / 512.732.0002

Melissa Gaskill: melissa@mansiongrovehouse.com

Consumer Copies:

Go to MansionGroveHouse.com for a current list of retailers and discount offers for copies of *Lacrosse: A Guide for Parents and Players*. Also available through leading chain and independent bookstores, online retailers, lacrosse pro shops, sporting goods stores, and catalogs.

Visit

MansionGroveHouse.com

Reseller Copies:

Distributor, Retailer & Lacrosse Group Inquiries to:

- ✓ Website: mansiongrovehouse.com
- ✓ Email: sales@mansiongrovehouse.com
- ✓ Phone: 408.404.7277
- ✓ Fax: 408.404.7277

Big Smiling Series

RAISING BIG SMILING TENNIS KIDS

Whether you are a tennis playing parent or a parent curious about tennis, this book will empower you to raise kids who swing the tennis racket with as much aplomb as their happy smiles.

The best age to get your kid started in tennis. How to motivate kids to go back, practice after practice. When to focus exclusively on tennis. Save on lessons, find scholarships and sponsors. How to pursue a career in professional tennis. Gain insight into tennis organizations and agents. Have fun along the way at the best tennis camps and resorts.

ISBN 1932421114
2006 Second Edition

RAISING BIG SMILING SQUASH KIDS

Stanford University recently added Squash to its athletics, joining Yale and Cornell. Forbes magazine rates Squash as the number one sport for fitness. With courts and college programs springing up across the country, the opportunities for a first class education are enhanced like never before for the serious junior squash player.

Richard Millman, world-class coach and Georgetta Morque, a prolific sportswriter, offer a complete roadmap for parents, professionals and kids. The best age to get started in squash; how to motivate kids; the road to top colleges; and attractive career options. Plus: cultivating friendships, character building and achieving a lifetime of fitness.

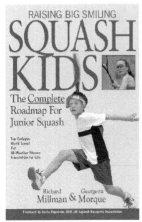

ISBN 1932421432
2006 First Edition

Available Worldwide

Made in the USA
Lexington, KY
04 April 2017